Dear Doodoo

I ʃ

Lor

You journey through using
your gifts for God's Kingdom!
Blessings! Emma
Eva Durgand

Creativity
in Us

MW01114120

EMMA BOA-DURGAMMAH

Creativity in Us

UNLEASH THE POWER OF GOD-GIVEN CREATIVITY

XULON PRESS

Xulon Press
2301 Lucien Way #415
Maitland, FL 32751
407.339.4217
www.xulonpress.com

© 2022 by Emma Boa-Durgammah
All rights reserved solely by the author. The author guarantees all contents are original and do not infringe upon the legal rights of any other person or work. No part of this book may be reproduced in any form without the permission of the author.
Due to the changing nature of the Internet, if there are any web addresses, links, or URLs included in this manuscript, these may have been altered and may no longer be accessible. The views and opinions shared in this book belong solely to the author and do not necessarily reflect those of the publisher. The publisher therefore disclaims responsibility for the views or opinions expressed within the work.

References to GOD, JESUS, CHRIST, HOLY SPIRIT, and LORD are intentionally in ALL CAPS.

Unless otherwise indicated, Scripture quotations taken from the Holy Bible, New International Version (NIV). Copyright © 1973, 1978, 1984, 2011 by Biblica, Inc.™. Used by permission. All rights reserved.
Paperback ISBN-13: 978-1-66286-794-1
Ebook ISBN-13: 978-1-66286-795-8

Dedication

This book is dedicated to:

- Anyone who has ever used a shopping cart;
- The countless individuals who have been discouraged from thinking their creativity mattered;
- The ones who have not felt empowered or equipped to live a lifestyle in which their creative gifts are applied in a wholesome way (e.g., professional, personal, and social life), and;
- Those who are an example of what it means to apply creativity in every aspect of life with consistency, urgency, and under the leadership of CHRIST.

Contents

Part III – LEADERSHIP, MINISTRY, and CREATIVE PRODUCTIVITY   133

Acknowledgments

A heartfelt thank-you to:

- The LORD, the Source of every human being and the Giver of all creative ability.
- My family: dad and mom - Francois and Sita for invaluable life lessons I will continuously cherish despite all odds; Winnie, Betty, and Frank Jr. for the incredible impact you continue to have and have had in my life as my biggest source of joy other than GOD, closest friends, and my rocks despite being stuck with me as your sibling.

A special thank you to Ms. Sylvia Taylor! Your teaching and encouragement mean the world to me. Knowing you prayed over me as one of your sixth-grade students before we entered your classroom warms my heart! I am a byproduct of your prayers and hope this encourages other teachers to lift their students in prayer. GOD used you to be the first Body of CHRIST member to build my GOD-Given creativity in more ways than you will ever know! I will forever be grateful for your witness!

A special thanks to the following who encouraged me directly or indirectly to write this book:

- Alyssa DeLutis-Hoethe; Andre Marks; Bob and Alicja Terzian; Bonnie Armstrong; Cameron Berner; Pastor Carolyn Brew; D'Erika Celosse; Derek and Damon Daniels; Pastor Dominic Knounbeke; Mother Emma Coles; Erik and Monica Sarmiento; Pastor Fred and Sister Zinnia Delarosa; Heather Maslonek; Pastor James and Katherine Lavender; Josh, Jamie, and Ben Johnson; Kathy Hoffman; Kristina and Michael Schenck; Kristy Siefkin; Dr. Kwasi Kena; Latoya and Corey Anderson; Mike, Kathy, Rachel, and Nathan Underhill; Misty Davis; Monsell Carter; Pamela Maida; Rick Brohaugh; my Rise Community Church Family; Ruth Barron; Pastors Shawn and Danell Perkins; Robin Portman; Shontya and Brian Washington; Silvana Barreda; Dr. Stephen and Dr. Feben Mobley; Sherrie Sawyer; Ms. Sylvia Taylor; and Dr. Tarik Phillip.

A special thanks to all clergy, lay ministers, friends, and current and past colleagues who have played instrumental roles in being the LORD's hands and feet in my life.

Endorsements

"Emma Boa-Durgammah does a masterful job in helping us discern our God-given creativity that is as unique as our fingerprint and points the way to the journey of discovery, discipline and destiny. This is a must-read book that will unleash your creativity! Get ready for an amazing ride!"

— **Danell Perkins,**
Senior Pastor, Rise Community Church

"I could not put down Creativity in Us!!! Emma Boa-Durgammah masterfully captures her readers with personal anecdotes and practical next steps. I am a medical professional who was convinced that I was not creative. However, this book has challenged me to engage in discovering my God-given creativity. More importantly, it has helped me realize the need to explore and encourage creativity in my children."

— **Dr. Feben Mobley,**
MD FACP, Internal Medicine

"Over two decades, I have watched Emma grow from a woman who simply loved and participated in the creative arts, to a Christ-centered leader who leverages creativity in every endeavor. As an entrepreneur, scholar, author, artist, and mentor, Emma shows us how harnessing our God-given creativity creates a life where possibilities are limitless.

Through Emma's book, I was called to rediscover the creativity that I feared had died inside of me. I left a secure, prestigious, and well-paying job to embrace my own God-given creative gifts as an entrepreneur. I have repeatedly turned to Emma's book for tactical and spiritual guidance as I navigate a new chapter. Every time I read it, I leave inspired and uplifted.

This book is a must-read for all who feel, 'there has to be more.' What a gift and blessing to have Emma as our guide as we use creativity to reach our highest potential."

— **Kristy Siefkin**,
Executive Communications Coach and
President of Kristy Siefkin Communications
https://kristysiefkin.com/;
Former journalist for CBS, Fox, Discovery, Animal Planet

"From the first page of the Introduction, Emma Boa-Durgammah presents Creativity in Us as a sacred invitation to live as co-creators with God. Being creative is a choice not reserved solely for those in the performing arts. No, creativity is for everyone regardless of vocation. Readers will quickly experience the author as a caring friend and confidant whose insights come from personal experience, purposeful study, and *intentional collaboration. After reading each chapter, you will find yourself saying, 'I can do this!' Read the entire book and you will know that creativity is a divine call not to be ignored."*

— **Dr. Kwasi Kena**,
Associate Professor of Ethnic and Multicultural Ministries, Wesley Seminary; Musician; Composer; Bible Story Performer

"In a world where 'innovation' has become a catchphrase or even maxim, Boa-Durgammah shows how God's gifts of creativity and innovation are inextricably linked! God's gifts of imagination and creativity, intentionally nurtured, greatly transform the human experience, and enable us to be all that God has created us to be."

— **Robin Portman**,
Executive Vice President for Corporate Growth, Booz Allen Hamilton (Retired); Former CEO and Board Chair, Atlas Research

Introduction

WHEN YOU HEAR THE WORD "CREATIVITY", do topics such as surgery, mathematical theorems, parenting, or social work come to mind? Probably not.

This book is an invitation to consider a shift in mindset and an alteration of habits. Creativity applies to every person and impacts every profession. Now more than ever, unleashing the power of GOD-Given creativity is needed as worldwide challenges present new complexities and nuances that the HOLY SPIRIT can lead us to address through GOD-Given creativity.

In the book, we will explore why creativity has been limited to certain fields. We will address why creativity lives in every person and needs to be exercised productively to live the Fulfilled, Actionable Creative Existence that helps us FACE and handle situations confident that we are made in the image of GOD.

Part I – The Time is Now, chapters one through seven, will address why unleashing the power of GOD-Given creativity is urgent. Individual and generational implications for holding back on applying GOD-Given creativity will be presented, along with the long-lasting impact it can have on everyone around you. We will also discover that creative productivity is fulfilling in all aspects of life and can be strategically planned and acted upon through the guidance of the LORD and a willingness to take bold steps to obey His leading.

Part II – How Do I Start, chapters eight through sixteen, will present practical concepts and tools you can creatively use to help you get started with consistently applying what GOD has entrusted unto you.

Part III – Leadership, Ministry, and Creative Productivity, chapters seventeen through twenty-one, will delve into the need and implementation dos and don'ts for creative productivity in leadership, evangelism, the larger Body of CHRIST, the local Church, and ministries. This section also contains a personal note from me, as a creative servant-leader (in my case, praise and worship arts) to other servant-leaders about our responsibility and the danger of burnout.

Finally, the appendix will provide an opportunity to start a plan to begin living the Fulfilled Actionable Creative Existence ("FACE") the LORD intended for you who are made in His image.

I included a few original songs and arrangements to accompany certain chapters within the book. I wrote and recorded some of these songs to the original instrumental beats that Monsell Carter created. You will learn more about this process in the upcoming chapters. When the chapter prompts you to listen to a specific song, please scan the image with your phone or visit https://linktr.ee/creativityinus. You will also find additional supporting materials on the website to deep-dive and integrate creative productivity into your lifestyle for GOD's Glory and the spread of His kingdom.

A special thanks to Monsell for the blessing of his witness as a young man-in-CHRIST, musical collaboration, and being willing to share his prayerful musical gift for creating beats for the Kingdom of GOD.

Part I

THE TIME IS NOW

CHAPTER 1:

ATTEMPTED MURDER vs. CREATIVITY

Why the Fulfilled Life Is Under Attack

The Enemy's Attempt

"THE ENEMY COMES TO STEAL, KILL, destroy..."[1] Every day, victims of attempted murder face a fresh twenty-four hours without an outlet for the creativity

---

[1] "John 10:10 (NIV)," *Bible Gateway,* last modified 2011, accessed December 5, 2022, https://www.biblegateway.com/passage/?search=John+10%3A10&version=NIV.

that exists in them. This creativity was gifted by GOD to be used often and productively for His kingdom. Yet, it is often the easiest thing to push aside, hold, or forego entirely. How is this happening and why is this significant at all? Scan below with your phone consider the first poem about a teacher, parent, and social worker which is presented in spoken word.

01 - "What a Shame" ©2022
Spoken word written and performed by Emma
Boa-Durgammah
Instrumental beats composed by Monsell Carter
Recording by Monsell Carter

Scan below or visit
https: //linktr.ee/creativityinus to hear this song

POEM 1 -
The Teacher / Parent / Social Worker

INTRO
Tic… Toc… Tic Toc

CHORUS
Joy was stolen.
Plans, destroyed.
Visions, murdered.
Enemy's plans furthered.
Enemy's plans furthered.
What a Shame!

STANZA 1
Teacher, parent, social worker, fried.
Long hours, sour, creativity denied.
They had "no time", they testified.
"What a shame!", they testified.

STANZA 2
Vibrant creatives in various ways.
Open mic nights, the lights, the pottery phase,
Long lost were all those days!
All those days!

STANZA 3
There was no point in wanting more!
That's what paying to watch the arts was for.
Being productive creatives was not in store,
Was not in store.

CHORUS
Their joy was stolen.
Plans, destroyed.
Visions, murdered.
Enemy's plans furthered.
Enemy's plans furthered.
What a shame!

POEM 2 -
The Dancer / Musician / Songwriter

Joy was stolen.
Plans, destroyed.
Visions, murdered.
Enemy's plans furthered.

A dancer, musician, songwriter abandoned their gifts and attires.
Would they ever dance, sing, write they wondered?
That career path was far from being pondered.

Concerned parents and friends ripped their dreams into shreds.
"Grow up!" those around them said.
Dreams did not pay bills "so let them be dead!"

The creatives were rattled.
Inside their souls embattled.
Despite their society-approved roles and perfect titles.

Dancer became lawyer, musician became doctor, songwriter
became marketer.
Roles that passed the litmus test of nay-sayers.
Roles that purportedly provided better bread and butter.

Joy was stolen.
Plans, destroyed.
Visions, murdered.
Enemy's plans furthered.

POEM 3 -
The Martial Artist / The Playwright /
The Fine Artist

The martial artist, playwright, fine artist, wondered if their craft
was ready.
Would anyone want to watch them compete, see, read what they
deemed unsteady?
They all had been showered with compliments they wanted to
believe so badly.

Promises of tomorrow seemed like empty words.
All they could feel was their shattering sense of worth.
Doubt overwhelmed them and accused them of not doing
"real work."

A siloed sales role screamed "time to move on."
Time to own up these dreams were foregone.
Time to grow up while hopes are forlorn.

Joy was stolen.
Plans, destroyed.
Visions, murdered.
Enemy's plans furthered.

POEM 4 -
The Engineer / The Scientist / The Mathematician

Left brain, right brain – never shall the two meet!
Engineer, scientist, and mathematician in defeat
Perceive creativity as self-imposed deceit.

Cognitive dissonance is ever-present.
The three creatives were once more than decent
Yet, they siloed their creativity and hailed King
Logical Prudence.

The former creatives cocooned in their vocational silos
Mourned the flow of former thanks and kudos
For they feared the risk of seeming non-empirical and
"one of those."

Joy was stolen.
Plans, destroyed.
Visions, murdered.
Enemy's plans furthered.

Creativity in Us

Thankfully, there is good news. First, let me be clear. There is nothing wrong with any of the professions listed in the poems you read. They all require the use of GOD-Given creativity in addition to intelligence and choice. We will cover how creativity applies to fields society does not usually deem creative in the upcoming chapters of this book. However, what is wrong is placing limits on creativity in a way that only validates its use within certain fields like the performing arts. This mindset and habits we form around it results in missed opportunities to engage in the fulfilled actionable creative existence GOD designed for us for the sake of His kingdom.

JESUS in John 10:10 warned, "the enemy comes to steal, kill, destroy"[2]. In the examples above, the enemy attempted to murder what GOD birthed. GOD-Given creativity and its first use by a human being can be seen in the Bible as early as Genesis 2:19. GOD after creating the birds of the sky and creatures on the earth asked Adam to name all of them.[3] The LORD delegated a complex and large-scale project that would require: 1) communion with Him, and 2) the desire to apply both intelligence and creativity. What is amazing is that Adam and Eve's résumés were completely empty. Their prior work experience was sorely lacking. Take a look at the next image to consider their lack of credentials or prior experience.

---

[2] "John 10:10 (NIV)," *Bible Gateway,* last modified 2011, accessed December 5, 2022, https://www.biblegateway.com/passage/?search=John+10%3A10&version=NIV.

[3] "Genesis 2:19 (NIV)," *Bible Gateway,* last modified 2011, accessed December 5, 2022, https://www.biblegateway.com/passage/?search=Genesis+2%3A19&version=NIV.

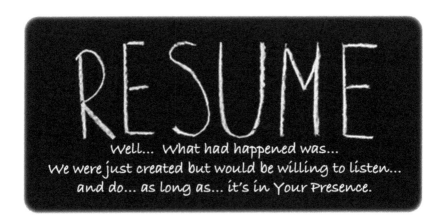

Why would GOD entrust them to partake in His Work when He could do it perfectly in the blink of an eye? Part of

Part of the design for life was for human beings to reflect the LORD in image, character, and creativity.

the design for life was for human beings to reflect the LORD in image, character, and creativity.[4] If we anchor in Him, commune with Him, and follow His leading, we fully partake in a mighty work beyond anything we could ever design or imagine that is not dependent on our résumés or credentials. We engage in work that has everlasting fulfilling fruit: the spread of His Good News, the building of His kingdom, and the partaking of the joyful and freeing identity and character we have in Him.

---

4 "Genesis 1:27-28 (NIV)," *Bible Gateway,* last modified 2011, accessed December 5, 2022, https://www.biblegateway.com/passage/?search=Genesis+1%3A27-28&version=NIV

10

It is not surprising the enemy tries to deceive us to forego one or more of the requirements for engaging in what GOD has called us to do. We are often tempted to exclusively use our intelligence or creativity, or commune with GOD without any follow-through or willingness to carry out the actions He leads. We, as the mirror image of GOD, all have the seed of creativity meant to be productively used for GOD's kingdom. If we allow Him to water this seed, it will produce impactful fruit and we will witness the power of applied, GOD-Given creativity. It is time for an overall shift in mindset and heart-set.

<u>Reflective Questions</u>

Which poem do you most relate to? If none, which poem would you write to best reflect your journey with creativity?

- ⇨ What are your biggest obstacles to engaging in the use of GOD-Given creativity daily?
- ⇨ What is accessible to you today to start integrating GOD-Given creativity daily?
- ⇨ Action Item - reach out to three friends or relatives who can hold you accountable for being more intentional about using your GOD-Given creativity. Next, set up a monthly or quarterly meeting to touch base with them.

CHAPTER 2:

THE SHOPPING CART

The Need for Daily Creativity

From Useless Idea to Household Staple

WHEN WAS THE LAST TIME YOU USED A
shopping cart? Can you imagine a world where a shopping

cart was considered a useless idea? Sylvan Nathan Goldman, the inventor of the shopping cart can. A son of a businessman from Oklahoma, he came up with the idea while thinking about the cumbersome metal shopping baskets people used when getting groceries at the food market and a folding chair in his office.[5]

Goldman had a mindset that did not dismiss his GOD-Given creativity and the possibility that viable candidates for creative solutions could be a chair or a basket. This allowed him to perceive a problem within the common practice of shopping and to believe he could come up with a solution.

Can you imagine a world where a shopping cart was considered a useless idea?

Engaging your GOD-Given creativity daily provides the confidence to find ways to take on challenges that may not yet be perceived as challenges. You can have an impact regardless of someone asking you to take action. On the surface, Goldman was bold enough to identify an inconvenience and had the confidence to believe he had everything at his disposal to provide a solution. At the core, Goldman was an astute man of faith who was applying creative productivity to every aspect of his life.

Goldman proceeded to install wheels on a folding chair and glue it to a metal cart. Voila! The first prototype was birthed. One would assume this would have been an instant relief for

---

[5] Modern Marvels, "Modern Marvels: How Supermarkets Operate (S13, E52)", Accessed August 1, 2022, https://www.youtube.com/watch?v=21FOQWtbyuA.

shoppers. One would imagine Goldman's rich and productive life would be evident and impactful as soon as this invention was launched. That could not have been further from the truth.

Don't Wait for Permission or Recognition to Use Your Creativity

It took ten years for the people in Goldman's circle to adopt the shopping cart as an integral part of their life. The initial paraphrased reaction from women was - why would I want to push something else around when I already have to push my baby from place to place? The initial paraphrased reaction from men was - do you think I'm not strong enough to carry a metal basket? Their myopic view of the world prevented them from partaking in the joy of being one of the first adopters of a significant and novel innovation.

Nevertheless, Goldman persevered and furthered his use of creativity to market the shopping cart despite opposition. He believed his contribution was worth promoting. Despite discouragement, he stayed the course and hired people to push shopping carts in stores and parking lots so he could inform shoppers entering the store about his invention and why it was integral to their shopping experience. More shoppers started using the cart, and the rest is history.

How many times have you backed away from using your creativity as a result of naysayers' opinions or self-doubt? We can glean some powerful lessons from someone history refers to as an inventor but who, in his early days, was not considered an authoritative voice in innovative spaces.

Others may not have known the shopping cart was the inception of a line of inventions that are still being used throughout the retail industry today. However, GOD did. The start of Goldman's creativity was the Source of all creation, the LORD GOD who had enabled him to have that seed of creativity as He was making him in His image. This is not limited to Goldman. GOD has already posited creativity in you! What is your shopping cart-like invention waiting to be birthed as GOD wills it?

Goldman ended up with multiple streams of creative productivity throughout his life, a concept we will explore further in this book, including becoming the president of the Super Market Institute, the vice-president of the International Food Congress, the vice-president of the National Association of Food Chains, a significant contributor to the arts, religious works, and the Southwest Center for Human Relations Studies at the University of Oklahoma, to name a few of his roles.

Another Present-Day Example

Anyone who knows my mom Sita, knows that flowers and gourmet cooking might as well have been her middle name. Ever since I can remember my mother has had the remarkable ability to turn certain items many would consider dying or useless, into beauty beyond recognition. She recently encountered a bike and flowerpots that were discarded in a junk pile. She painted them and planted dying flowers within to revive them using her GOD-Given creativity. She then did the same for the cube. This next image portrays the final product.

Her flowers have been a consistent point of attraction. I can't recall the number of times people have stopped to ask about her secret. The point is that mom recognized value in the seemingly useless. Her confidence in her ability to creatively restore the devalued has blessed many.

What would it look like for each person to revisit what they have discarded and labeled consciously or subconsciously unusable? Think about how many could be impacted by our proactive use of the gifts the LORD has entrusted to us.

You and I cannot afford to neglect creativity as a gift that ought to be opened, utilized, and fostered daily, as guided by the Source of all creation, the LORD GOD.

One More Example

If you listened to the song in chapter one of this book, you heard one of the many beats that my friend Monsell Carter casually made, just because! He mentioned in passing that he was dabbling with making beats after a praise and worship rehearsal where he was serving as part of the Audio/

Visual team at my home Church, Rise Community Church. I expressed that I would love to listen to one of his beats if he was comfortable because I was curious. He seemed hesitant, and he expressed it was a scratch version. Nevertheless, he took a leap of faith for which I am grateful. What he did not know is that the excuses he was giving me were the same I did for years because I never felt my songs were "good enough" or "valuable enough" to finalize. I have since tried to encourage other musicians to use their gifts for GOD's Kingdom.

After hearing how gifted he was, I prayed, then invited him to collaborate by choosing a few beats he liked and was willing to share in the context of this book. I, in turn, would see which ones could fit into songs I was writing or had already written but never officially published or released. Check out a screenshot of the first leap of faith he took in the next image.

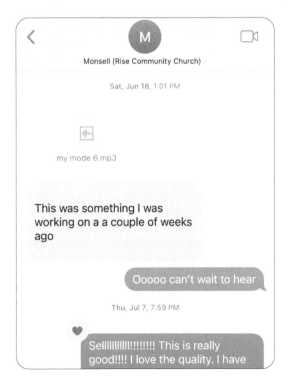

The outcome of this leap of faith was that the LORD allowed us to generate the songs you will hear throughout the book. They are intended to enhance your experience of the content and prayerfully encourage you to take action.

Avoid the Expensive Compromise

It would have been too expensive to the world to lose the contributions of Sylvan Nathan Goodman, my mom, and Monsell Carter because of self-doubt or any other obstacles to creative productivity. I am glad the enemy did not win in these cases. If you are facing some obstacles to your productive creativity, you will want to keep reading. Be encouraged and know your silence is more expensive and harmful in the long run than your faith. Dare to take the first leap toward unleashing the power of GOD-Given creativity in you!

CHAPTER 3:

POWER UP YOUR CREATIVITY

Choose the Fulfilled, Actionable Creative Existence

<u>Creative Productivity Defined</u>

TO PROPERLY UNDERSTAND WHY unleashing GOD-Given creativity is important, we need to begin with the definition of creative productivity.

Creativity productivity impacts others and advances GOD's kingdom as a byproduct of your identity in CHRIST. Creativity can be elating but by itself can never lead to an experience of a <u>F</u>ulfilled <u>A</u>ctionable <u>C</u>reative <u>E</u>xistence ("FACE") in the image of GOD, which we will cover in this book.

<u>Why Is Creative Productivity Powerful?</u>

Do you know that creative thinking leverages both hemispheres of the brain? If you are a believer-in-CHRIST, you know He created you and therefore is the true Source, Revealer, and Activator of the creativity He instilled in you. Only He can guide how your gifts can become productive for the sake of His kingdom. Therefore, you can freely reflect His image in your daily methods of expression and experience a fulfilled and creative existence. This is the position of most impact and joy.

> **"**
>
> *Creative Productivity = Using Your Gifts, Skills, and Tools to Glorify GOD*
>
> **"**

If you are a potential believer-in-CHRIST or are on the fence but can relate to being discouraged from integrating creativity in your life, please be encouraged to persevere with the gifts you possess because they can impact others around you. Say yes to the invitation CHRIST is extending to you as you read this book and watch Him take that creativity to powerful and impactful depth as you take action. My prayer and commitment to you as an author is that I will continue to pray that one day you will allow CHRIST to guide your heart so that you know how to best use your gifts for His Glory.

<u>The Rise of Hope!</u>

Thankfully, the stories in the first chapter are not over! Every role from the mathematician to the dancer is intrinsically comprised of opportunities for a Fulfilled Actionable Creative Existence ("FACE"). How does someone partake in the FACE lifestyle? In Isaiah 60, Israel had been under attack and in response had built walls and locked gates to defend itself. In verse 18, Isaiah prays that the LORD will transform the walls that had been built as defense into the emblem of recognition about how the LORD saves. He also prays for the gates that were created to keep the enemy out to be transformed into praise and remembrance of GOD coming to their defense and defeating the enemy. Some of us have built walls in our hearts and locked the gate to our dreams as the enemy attempted to murder what GOD birthed. Visit https://linktr.ee/creativityinus. To engage in the FACE journey, know that GOD can thwart the violent attacks of the enemy against the gifts He entrusted unto you so you can arise victoriously and best represent Him.[6] Therefore, trust Him to unlock His will in your life. Partake in the Fulfilled Actionable Creative Existence He has designed for you. He will continuously provide what you need if you align yourself with doing His will. I invite you to listen to the following song I wrote to the instrumental beat Monsell created.

---

[6] "Isaiah 60:18 (NIV)," *Bible Gateway,* last modified 2011, accessed December 5, 2022, https://www.biblegateway.com/passage/?search=Isaiah+60%3A18&version=NIV.

02 - "Purpose in Your Name" ©2022
Vocal music and lyrics written and performed by Emma
Boa-Durgammah
Instrumental beats composed by Monsell Carter
Recording by Monsell Carter

Scan or visit
https://linktr.ee/creativityinus to hear this song

INTRO
Isaiah 60:18, GOD, You changed their gates to praise
In Isaiah 60:18, GOD, You broke their walls, made a way!
In the glory of Your passion, can You change my gates
to praise?
Will You become my salvation?
Can You break my walls?
Can You make a way?

VERSE
The sun came down on all my plans
My heart's content comes to, to an end
I built up walls and took my stance
I did not want to take a second chance

PRE-CHORUS

My gates are locked, let my dreams just end
I won't get hurt, these walls are my defense
These walls extend toward heaven

CHORUS

Make my walls Salvation, change my gates to Praise
Fill my life with purpose, purpose in Your Name
Use me as a vessel, use my life Your Way
Fill my life with purpose, purpose in Your Name
Your Holy Name – JESUS

VERSE

Creative doors are part of Your Plans
Internal walls… fall in the Palm of Your Hands
Gates unlock so Your Will extends
I don't get hurt, because You are my Defense
Your Will extends… from earth to heaven

CHORUS

Make my walls Salvation, change my gates to Praise
Fill my life with purpose, purpose in Your Name
Use me as a vessel, use my life Your Way
Fill my life with purpose, LORD
Purpose in Your Name

CHORUS

Make my walls Salvation, change my gates to Praise
Fill my life with purpose, purpose in Your Name
Use me as a vessel, use my life Your Way
Fill my life with purpose, LORD
Purpose in Your Name
Your Holy Name – JESUS – Your Holy Name

<u>Closing Prayer</u>

LORD, make our walls salvation and our gates praise. Teach us to revisit the ways You created us to be creatively productive. Allow us to leverage the creativity You entrusted unto us for the sake of Your glory. Reveal what is already on our table and accessible for such a time as this. Thank You for Your provision, path to creative productivity, guidance about the next steps, and for providing us with the choice to engage in a fulfilled, actionable creative existence. Amen!

CHAPTER 4:

HELP THE GENERATIONS GROW!

What We Do Today Impacts Generations to Come

The Joy of Ingenuity, Creativity, and Engineering

WHEN I THINK ABOUT GENERATIONAL impact, I am reminded of the movie "Joy".[7] In the movie, Joy's grandmother, recalls her granddaughter's younger days as an inventor. At a young age, Joy invented and engineered a dog collar that had a quick release. Nothing ever happened

---

[7] *Joy*, directed by David O Russell (20th Century Fox, 2015), 2:04:00.

with her inventions because her parents did not commit to encouraging her to continue to use her creativity. In a later scene in the movie, Joy turns to her mom and reproaches her, stating that she could have been successful because a company that invented the same thing years after she did held the patent on the invention. In the scene, Joy is portrayed as barely being able to make ends meet. Her mom responds that she didn't know any better and much less about patents.

To be fair, the period portrayed in the movie was not one of modern conveniences such as cell phones or expedient research tools like the internet. However, it is possible her mom did not value this gift enough to inquire about ways to further her child's invention. This scene depicts a young Joy crying out to her mom for validation. Instead, her mom responds with silence. Frustrated, young Joy must grow up quickly and figure out on her own what to do with the inventions she ideated. For years, she resolves to let her dreams die.

Generational Encourager

Thankfully in the movie, Joy's grandmother astutely kept encouraging her creativity. Even when things failed, she let Joy know she was gifted and destined to be successful and restore the whole family. She was right! Joy became successful through her no-touch, machine-washable, durable cotton mop and created over 100 additional inventions thereafter. Joy broke the cycle of repressed and unused creativity and flourished with ingenuity and engineering. The application of her GOD-Given creativity contributed to her personal success and her family's prosperity.

I often wonder how many people like Joy are one generational encourager away from being able to unleash the power of their GOD-Given creativity. I also ponder the number of generational encouragers who do not feel they can speak into others' lives because they do not value their critical role. If that is you, your silence is too expensive. It is time to boldly step into the role GOD has for you.

The next song I wrote to Monsell's instrumental beats represents the heartfelt cry from generations today who need more generational encouragers to arise and act. Will you be next?

03 - "Help the Generations Grow" ©2022
Vocal music and lyrics written and performed by Emma
Boa-Durgammah
Instrumental beats composed by Monsell Carter
Recording by Monsell Carter

Scan or visit
https://linktr.ee/creativityinus to hear this song

INTRO
[Ugh! – sounds of frustration]
Help! Help! Help! Help!
Why won't you just help?

VERSE 1
Mama, daddy, help me!
Grandpa, granny hold me!
Don't throw me silence
Embrace the hours that move and inspire!
Why am I leaning
All on my own though I love creating
And ideating?

CHORUS
Help the generations grow!

VERSE 2
Friends and colleagues, help me!
Mentors, don't desert me!
Don't throw me silence
Embrace the hours that move and inspire!
Why am I leaning
All on my own though I love creating
And ideating?

CHORUS
Help the generations grow!

BRIDGE 1
Momma and Daddy throw me the
Si---lence
Sever the hours that move and inspire
I'm running from this misunderstanding, misundertanding.
Momma and Daddy throw me the
Si---lence
Sever the hours that move and inspire
I'm running from this misunderstanding.

BRIDGE 2
Don't give up!
Don't give in!
Let gifts flow!
Let the generations grow!

BRIDGE 3

Rebuke the doubter
For he has no power
To overcome what
GOD has inspired, empowered this hour, I'll grow!

BRIDGE 3

I rebuke the doubter
For he has no power
To overcome what
GOD has inspired, empowered this hour, I'll grow!

BRIDGE 2

Don't give up!
Don't give in!
Let gifts flow!

CHORUS

Let the generations grow!

BRIDGE 2

Don't give up!
Don't give in!
Let gifts flow!

CHORUS

Help the generations grow!

ENDING
Help the generations grow!
Help the generations grow!
Let gifts flow!
Help the generations grow!

<u>Generational Hope in CHRIST</u>

I remember sitting down to watch the sunset on a visit to Brookfield Greens Garden in South Carolina when a photographer came over and mentioned that a proposal was about to take place. She asked if I would mind moving over. I gladly got up. She ran to her position to take the picture and while she did, another couple was about to sit down in the same spot I was asked to keep clear. I went over to the couple and shared the news with them, and they got up.

I then decided to sit there so I could prevent anyone from making the same mistake. My instructions from the photographer were to plan to move when the soon-to-be-engaged couple approached. I glanced behind me and got a thumbs up from the people sitting on the bench behind me. I gave them a thumbs up as well thinking they were family members of the engaged couple.

Don't give in!
Let gifts flow
Help the
generations grow!

Suddenly, we all heard huge cheers close by. We looked at each other and said: did we miss it? That's when I officially met the people behind me and discovered they were just bystanders like me who were excited to partake in the surprise engagement. When we heard the cheers, we all felt somewhat disappointed because as we suspected, the groom had decided to propose 100 feet away from us. If he had proposed right in front of us, we would have been elated at the moment we'd had a hand in creating however minuscule the part.

Choosing to use creativity to partake in the plans GOD has for us to expand His Kingdom can provide a life of wholesome abundance from the inside out. We get to cheer others' successes and our own, overcome the elements that threaten to thwart progress for His Kingdom, and course-correct as needed, which in turn results in creative productivity. It can feel like being a part of GOD's proposal to people to choose a lifestyle of covenant with Him. Choosing to use creativity as we please can still be engaging and even temporarily fulfilling. However, this dissipates over time, especially once the accolades and recognition dwindle or our sense of perfectionism produces the type of analysis paralysis that halts progress. It can be the equivalent of hearing cheers but not getting to fully partake in the resulting moment of engagement. The wholesome abundant life in JESUS adds an incredible dimension to the use of creativity. Moreover, GOD is a GOD of order and helps us to take action toward creative productivity.

When it comes to generational creative productivity, please consider inviting CHRIST to guide the gifts He has entrusted to you to affect generations to come. Please hear my heart, I am not referring to an inability to be successful in your creative endeavors but rather never being able to experience the fulfilled, actionable creative existence only CHRIST can provide. Will you consider allowing Him to impact future generations to come starting with you today?

<u>Identify the State of Generational Creative Productivity in Your Life</u>

1. Pray.
2. Please note digitally or on in writing, anyone in your family lineage whom you have noticed seems to enjoy the gifts of creating and ideating. Include relatives from both parents if you know them.
3. Write down the ones in your response to the previous question who used and shared their gifts with others.
4. Write down the ones that passed on their gifts intentionally.
5. Write down the ones who worked on their gifts but never shared them with others or constantly questioned if their gifts were valid or worthy of sharing.
6. Have a conversation with the ones who doubted their gifts and did not share and ask the following questions
   a. Why not. Document their response.
   b. Would they consider starting now. Document their response.
   c. Safekeep or bookmark this important tool for you to access and avoid going down the same path in the future.
7. Provide a copy of this book to those who did not share their gifts and encourage them to start now.

8. Note your insights from this generational creative productivity exercise.
9. Note the gifts you are engaged in, are sharing and why.
10. Note the gifts you are not sharing or have abandoned and why.
11. Note your insights from the lists you created about your creative productivity in questions 9 and 10.
12. Compare your creative productivity responses to the generational ones from others in your family.
    a. Note similarities
    b. Note differences
    c. Note trends. Has your lineage been engaging in creative productivity for generations? Do you have the blessing of being the first?
13. Capture the gifts you would like to start using and sharing that you have not shared to date.

Become the one who resists the enemy's generational attempted murder of creative productivity in your family lineages.

CHAPTER 5:

BREAKING NEWS!!!

Creativity Can Exist in Any Profession

WHEN I ENCOUNTER PEOPLE IN professional, social, and religious circles I can usually tell when someone believes that they are creative at heart. It seems that creativity has often been relegated to a handful of fields such as the fine arts (e.g., painting, sketching) or the performing arts (e.g., music, dance). Where else could creativity be inconspicuously occurring and impactful? This chapter will explore the answers to these questions.

<u>Socially Unrecognized Creativity</u>

In the next table, I am including a few examples where creativity is not often mentioned as a requirement, albeit its presence and applicability. Creativity is what someone has to use when there are multiple approaches to implementing the role. There are countless fields where creativity is intricately in effect. The following table is based on fields in which my immediate circle of family, friends, and colleagues work.

Role	Creativity Highlight
Water resources engineer	Creatively decipher the most optimal tools to convey, route, store, or release fluid as each situation demands. (A special thanks to my wonderful sister, Winnie for this one!)
Parent (Stay-at Home or Multi-Vocational	Creatively generate unique plans of action to raise, educate, encourage, challenge, and unconditionally love each child in light of their individual personality, character, and behavioral style.
Data analyst	Creatively synthesize volumes of data and facts into actionable steps that will help meet a goal.
Sales/Solutions engineer	Creatively discern applicable solutions to solve client's pain points. Devise an effective communication plan that tends to each client's unique need.
Environmental engineer	Creatively perceive ways in which remedies can be applied to environmental challenges.
Financial planner	Creatively devise plans of action to help people meet their financial goals.
Fitness instructor	Creatively find ways to address fitness challenges in a fun and accessible way that caters to a variety of fitness levels.
Mathematician	Creatively devise a method to solve an unresolved problem.
News anchor	Assess the news and creatively deliver the information in digestible morsels for viewers.
Process engineer	Creatively perceive the potential for processes in the absence of order or systems.
Scientist	Creatively develop methods to make discoveries and apply them to fill gaps where needed.
Medical Professional	Creatively synthesize the information from patients against objective findings to resolve their illnesses.
Social worker	Creatively decipher which resources will best help clients and communicate effectively with each to achieve restoration.
Software engineer	Employ creativity in imagining both functionality and output regardless of specifications being clearly defined.
Teacher	Creatively generate and administer effective learning methods to help learners intake the information you need to convey.
[Insert Role]	[You will find areas where creativity applies]

Socially Recognized Creativity

The following are a few examples of creativity where the word is frequently mentioned. This is based on my immediate circle of friends or colleagues.

Role	Creativity Highlight
Musician	Creatively express a message using music and applicable instruments and tools.
Choreographer	Creatively develop patterns of movement considering various dance levels and dancers' capacity to move in the way you envision and adapt to inspire a cohesive performance.
Craftsmen	Creatively transform raw materials into works of art.
Dancer	Creatively use your body for artistic expression.
Instrumentalist	Creatively use your instrument to convey music and draw reactions.
Jewelry artist	Creatively select and combine materials to generate wearable art.
Mime dancer	Creatively use motions to silently, yet boldly express emotions or scenarios.
Music Director	Creatively devise lesson plans and methods to get musicians prepared to present their craft.
Painter	Creatively capture on paper, canvas, or other forms expressions of life or new imagined ideas and transform them into art.
Poet	Creatively use words to convey imagery or what needs to be expressed.
Sketch Artist	Creatively capture life using pencil and paper or other formats, ensuring three-dimensional forms are captured despite two-dimensional nature of the art format.
Songwriter	Creatively generate original or arranged music and lyrics to express situations, emotions, life, or expectations.

<u>Creativity Is Not Siloed to Certain Fields</u>

The examples provided are not intended to represent all the fields where creativity takes place every day nor purport to cover all the ways creativity exists within those fields. However, my prayer is that the above samples help you to understand creativity can exist in all professions.

<u>Partnering to Unleash Creativity</u>

An effective way to further creative productivity is to partner with other individuals who have already engaged in it or have a desire to do so. When considering a partnership, I recommend you ensure the person 1) has the drive and desire to be creatively productive; 2) will be a complement to what you have to offer and not be intimidated by you or vice versa; 3) communicates either in a similar fashion or understands *and* accepts your communication style; and 4) is willing to stay centered on a mission over personal agenda. Creative productivity can work well if the partners effectively collaborate for the right reasons. I have been very blessed to partner with my sister-in-CHRIST Kristina Schenck in other endeavors who embodies the above.

Getting Started – Current Creative Productivity in Your Life

⇨ What layers of creativity do you engage in every day?

o Identify which fields or spaces.

⇨ How are you using your creativity to expand GOD's Kingdom?

⇨ With whom can you partner to further your creative productivity?

CHAPTER 6:

KNOCK KNOCK...

Open the Door to Multiple Streams of Productivity

The Importance of Having Streams of Creative Productivity

YOU MAY HAVE HEARD PEOPLE SAY IT IS important to have various streams of income. The reason is that continued financial stability is more likely when someone has multiple sources of income. If one stream of income fails, the others can sustain the person financially. I would like to submit that it is more important to start with various streams of productivity.

A stream of productivity is a role where you use GOD-Given creativity frequently, preferably every day. The same reason applied to streams of income holds true for productivity. An additional benefit is that various streams of productivity provide a pathway to sustainable creative productivity and can be a potent precursor to holistic and sustainable streams of income. Examples of streams of productivity can be your workplace, marriage, single friends' group, weekend soccer team, ministry, and mentorship, among many others.

It is important to note that one can have various streams of income yet still be unfulfilled. When considering possible streams of income, if you start with prayer, GOD reveals what will creatively produce in a way that is fulfilling. More importantly, you will have building blocks to help you withstand adversity when one stream of productivity is under attack.

Choosing Streams of Creative Productivity to Undertake

The first step is knowing when to say "no." The second step is embracing that each "no" allows you to make room for "yeses" with impact. People have often asked me if I know how to say the word "no." They evaluate what they see on the surface and assume that I just undertake whatever comes my way. However, I reject most offers to engage in projects far more than what I undertake. I admit I am not always right in my yeses but am increasingly learning to weigh faster the cost of saying yes without the leading of the HOLY SPIRIT. These "nos" have been intentional and have made room for the yeses that contribute to various streams of productivity in my life today, including this book. GOD has continuously sustained what He has led, even when if the implementation changed.

Make Room

I will never forget the day I entered my little room in a townhome I shared with three other friends years ago. I was greeted with a lovely surprise. My friend Heather, who was my roommate at the time, had snuck in a grey YPG235 Yamaha Portable Grand keyboard in the center of my cozy 9' x 9' room. My room was so small that it was clear my roommate had to make space so the keyboard could be the central piece when I walked in. This moment is permanently engraved in my mind.

Turning Point

A couple of weeks before I experienced Heather's surprise, she and I had a discussion that just seemed like a casual table conversation. We had been talking about different ways to capture original music when I am songwriting to avoid forgetting. I had learned some tricks along the way since I started writing music. Since I was six years old, original music (at times entire songs) would pop in my head: melody, harmonies, instruments, lyrics, everything. Other times, what I could hear was a melody and a couple of instruments. At six years old my parents gifted me with a little keyboard with two octaves.

I wrote my first instrumental piece using this keyboard but I did not know how to record enough of what the LORD was gifting me to create before the next one popped in my head, or I began arranging the one I was writing in my head. I did not know how to read music, nor had I had piano lessons. I tried to remember as much as I could, but without an outlet to record or capture what I was writing, many original songs from age six to high school were lost in the abyss of my memory.

When I was older, I learned different tools like recording components of a song on my phone, along with their thematic chord progression which I would hum into my phone. I researched basic ways to record and learned audio layering with free software like Audacity to conceptually capture enough of my originals. I knew having a keyboard with decent sounds would enable me to add drums and could be a game changer.

I was just shooting the breeze when I mentioned it casually in my conversation with Heather. Who knew she had not only been listening but actively resolving to be GOD's hands and feet to me at that moment? Her keyboard gift, by the leading of GOD, was a turning point for me to actively partake in the power of the creativity He posited in me.

The Power of Listening to Others and Engaging in Calculated Empowerment

What Heather's gift symbolized was that my shooting-the-breeze mindset and heart-set about the gift of creativity GOD entrusted unto me needed to shift so I could use it for His Glory. Her GOD-inspired gift enhanced one of my streams of productivity, using music to spread the Gospel.

Shortly after I received Heather's gift, a sister-in-CHRIST asked me to lead a worship night by singing and playing music simultaneously. My sister and ministry partner-in-CHRIST Kristina who co-founded the Worship Arts Production® ministry Keyedin-2 CHRIST with me, can attest to the fact that before this invite, playing and singing simultaneously was very difficult for me. I know I'm about to sound crazy but my "yes," in combination with being intentional and ready to serve GOD through the gifts He had imparted to me, led to a miracle. GOD unlocked my fingers so I could play and sing simultaneously for the worship night and thereafter.

Creatively FACE Opposition

Making room for our gifts will result in an impact that inevitably will contribute to a Fulfilled Actionable, Creative Existence. This lifestyle enables you to take heart and withstand times of adversity or even sabotage from others.

I recently had a situation with one of my streams of productivity where an individual was spreading lies against me. This was disappointing because it quickly became a difficult space to navigate. The incident could have been soul-crushing outside of this GOD-Inspired journey comprised of multiple streams of creative productivity. However, by the Grace of GOD, it did not consume me in all areas of my life.

To be clear, I was very affected. However, I was still content overall because 1) GOD is Steadfast and was gifting me with breath every day so I could continue to serve Him and 2) the impact He was having in and through me in the other streams of productivity in which I was engaged continued forward. Having a variety in your streams of productivity under the leadership of the HOLY SPIRIT can help you persevere through the unexpected. It provides remembrance for the beautifully and wonderfully made person He has designed you to be.

Having a variety in your streams of productivity under the leadership of the HOLY SPIRIT can help you persevere when one stream becomes less stable.

It helps you to courageously advocate for yourself regardless of people's misconstrued notions about you. It also safely allows you to let go of your agenda and let GOD work out painful situations in His time. In my case, the resolution to the situation where my stream of productivity became challenging, was better than I could have ever expected, and it holds the promise of becoming a better stream of productivity today.

Steps toward Making Room for GOD-Given Creativity

⇨ List your current streams of productivity.

⇨ Acknowledge the LORD has created you to be creatively productive.

    o It is the fabric of who you are therefore don't allow the enemy to distract you from engaging in whom the LORD has made you to be.

⇨ Prayerfully determine and list what needs to come off your table so you can engage in daily creativity.

⇨ Start to pause and appreciate what you creatively bring to the table. Note what you are bringing to the table today.

⇨ Identify places where you have not integrated creativity.

    o Don't neglect workplaces, social, personal, religious, interpersonal, and economic spaces, among others.

⇨ Carve ten minutes out of your day to integrate creativity and determine a start date.

⇨ Share your plan of action with one other person who will hold you accountable.

CHAPTER 7:

CHICKEN SOUP PLEASE!

Healing through Creative Productivity, Grief, and My Personal Testimony

IT IS TIME FOR A CONFESSION ON MY part. On one hand, this chapter has nothing to do with chicken soup, but many times when I think of healing, I think of chicken soup. On the other hand, this chapter has everything to do with how GOD can heal through creative productivity. I would like to start with a part of my testimony.

Her creative productivity, because she was submitted unto GOD, sparked the flame I needed to heal, and proceed in my new life and calling.

My Background

The cold air permeated my skin and sank into my inner core as I consciously began a new life in unfamiliar territory. It was seventy degrees, and I was freezing! How did I end up here at eleven years old?

Her creative productivity, because she was submitted unto GOD, sparked the flame I needed to heal, and proceed in my new life and calling.

My life until then had been predictable, stable, and a respite. I was privileged to experience the benefits of money, parental affection, a stellar private-school education, and cultural exposure at a young age. I had a life any young girl might have wanted.

Born and raised in the metropolitan city of Abidjan, in Cote D'Ivoire, a French-speaking country in the continent of Africa (no…Africa is not a country), I attended Notre Dame, an all-girls Catholic school. I came to the United States at a very young age for a couple of years with my parents but barely remembered this season of my life. The majority of my memories until eleven are from Cote D'Ivoire.

The daily routine was rather mundane: get up, put on the private Catholic school uniform, and get a ride to school. Once in school, I faced the rigors of a rigid curriculum, occasionally misbehaved, and was reprimanded in various ways, including corporal punishment. After a morning of learning, we would eat lunch, nap, and continue the day's lessons. On weekends, we would visit the fun-filled beaches of Grand Bassam, ensuring we paid a visit to Uncle Marcel, who owned an exceptional grill on the beach. The fish was fresh. The meat was succulent. The waves were refreshing beneath the hot sun of the equatorial city of Abidjan. It seemed like an ideal life by many people's standards.

However, this was the time where my GOD-Given gift for music was attacked. I was told I did not have a good voice in school and could, at best, just sing background. Unfortunately, I profoundly internalized this critique.

<u>My Parents Rock the Boat</u>

At eleven, my parents decided to move to the United States. I was devastated! I was especially panicked about leaving my buddies Natalie, Vassili, Jerome, Frédérique, and Jean-François. We had grown up together and were practically family. The entire foundation for who I was, what I thought I would be and do, had been built in Abidjan, and people knew who I was!

Moreover, I had just accepted CHRIST as my Savior when during a timeout, I defiantly opened the only Book available in my room, the Bible. Well, the joke was on me! The LORD captured my heart that day. What would faith mean in America? I had more questions than answers. That did not matter. I did not have a choice. My parents had already made up their minds. I hopped on a plane with my parents, and my two younger sisters, Betty, and Winnie. I was convinced my parents had made a terrible mistake!

Nevertheless, here we were in the late summer, landing in the United States to approximately seventy-degree weather. I was bundled in a bubble jacket because the cold was unbearable. Cote D'Ivoire was consistently a familiar eighty to ninety degrees Fahrenheit, so the cool breeze of Virginia felt like the blistery blizzard wind of the Icelandic icecaps. We headed to the McDonalds next to the Breezeway Motel in Fairfax, and twenty-seven dollars later had indulged in the Golden Arch's most refined breakfast and *"were lovin' it!"* Yes, we were fresh off the plane and did not know any better!

<u>Music as a Healing Tool GOD Used</u>

My first year in Vienna, Virginia, was difficult. I was embittered by the lack of choice I had in our move, was verbally bullied at school, had no friends for the majority of my first year in the U.S., and owned only two shirts, two pairs of jeans, and two nicer outfits. My version of being "dressed up" was my mom's selection of two outfits that emulated seventies attire and eyewear. Sixth-grade kids were brutally honest and flat-out mean at times. I walked to and from school in tears most days and, within a couple of months, had given up on even changing shirts every day. What was the point? They all hated me anyways!

Thankfully, through this, GOD still loved me and sent an intercessor in prayer, compassion, and encouragement to heal the gaping wounds in my heart. I had no idea the extent to which this was a GOD connection. My loving sixth-grade music teacher Ms. Sylvia Taylor was GOD's vessel for healing in multiple aspects I cannot fully and adequately describe. I was very grateful for Ms. Taylor because I was told I did not have a good singing voice in grade school prior to her. Yet, Ms. Taylor encouraged me to pursue music and gave me my first music award by the end of sixth grade. She encouraged me to continue writing songs and had the choir sing a piece I wrote entitled "You Gotta Believe."

All Rights Reserved

The lyrics I wrote in sixth grade were "you gotta believe in yourself and conquer all those fears, yeah you gotta believe in which you feel is just and right for this world." I could have never imagined seeds were being planted through Ms. Taylor's prayers so the lyrics as I would write them today have transformed into "you gotta believe in CHRIST the King who conquered over fear. Yes, you've gotta believe in what He leads. He holds all rights in this world." Her creative productivity, because she was submitted unto GOD, sparked the flame I needed to heal, and proceed in my new life and calling. Her obedience is in part why I can write this book at all today. She fundamentally understood that when a shift in mindset points to "all rights reserved for GOD," His work in and through people reaches far beyond what they can see.

During that time, I wrote songs as an outlet for emotional responses to life and to process rapid transitions in my life.

These songs became a powerful tool GOD used to heal me. I am including one of the pieces I started writing between the sixth and seventh grades in the throes of my mourning life expectations in the face of depressing transitions.

The song was finished decades later to give voice to those whose hope is fading and to encourage the Body of CHRIST to be attuned to the hurting, journey with them, and introduce them to CHRIST who is the lasting Hope in situations of hopelessness. The song is entitled "Something to Smile About." This is my live recording of the song.

04 - "Something to Smile About" ©2018
Music and lyrics written, performed, and recorded live by
Emma Boa-Durgammah

Scan or visit
https://linktr.ee/creativityinus to hear this song.

VERSE 1

Humor me; it's been a while
I built a fence to masquerade my life
If you take the chance
To climb over this fence
You will humor me

CHORUS

Give me something to smile about
Give me something to smile about

VERSE 2

Think of me; I'm screaming inside
My hope is faint; I'm dimming my light
I need a friend to understand my life
Who will humor me

CHORUS

Give me something to smile about
Give me something to smile about

BRIDGE

Give me something, give a smile
Though it may take a while
Though I can't smile back, you may just save my life
Show me JESUS through your life
Then break down this lie
That He gave up, that you gave up,
that His Body gave up on my life, my life

VERSE 3
Humor me, show me how CHRIST
Can be a friend who understands my life
Who took the chance to climb over this fence
Who will humor me

CHORUS
Give me something to smile about
Give me something to smile about

Creativity Outside of CHRIST vs. Creative Productivity in CHRIST

Seventh grade was off to a rocky start because we moved from Vienna to Fairfax, Virginia. I did not understand cultural norms, was still learning English, and had failed the Virginia literacy test a couple of times (despite having a mandatory requirement at home to watch or listen to two hours of American television or radio instead of signing up for English as a Second Language classes).

One morning I decided enough was enough. I combined my passion for music with my need to learn English. I started memorizing lyrics to hip-hop songs; the faster, the better. With an understanding of certain songs, I became friends with a few people, and before I knew it, was part of a group of friends. Perhaps rebuilding a community in the U.S. was possible! This country was starting to grow on me, despite my lack of choice in coming here. Engaging in creativity was temporarily helpful in that context. However, it pales in comparison to being able to do so to further GOD's kingdom.

When I Invited GOD to Take LORDship Over My Gifts

It is interesting to remember my journey with music. I was writing songs and original music in my head at the age of six. Though I sang occasionally, I did not feel that I had a gift or a good voice that could be shared. Music was a tool I was using to process and conceptualize life's highs and lows. This singular purpose for music drastically shifted when I asked GOD to take over the gift of singing and songwriting. This shift in my prayer life, along with a willingness to focus on deepening my relationship with CHRIST and follow His LORDship has enabled me to begin experiencing fullness in life and taking action toward living a creatively productive existence for His kingdom. It no longer mattered what I felt about my gift or vocal perfection. What mattered was that I was open to serving Him with the gift, tool, and skill of music. The more I am in relationship with CHRIST, the more fulfilling it gets to honor Him for Who He is, which results in more fulfillment from experiencing Him rather than outcomes from what He enables me to produce. This shift in what fulfills me is the core difference between using creativity and creative productivity powered by GOD.

GOD-Given Creativity Helps Heal Grief

I was the oldest of four siblings. My sister Betty, the second oldest sibling, was hilarious and sarcastic. I loved her dearly because she was battling seizures that were increasingly getting worse, but no one would have ever guessed because she took life so lightly. Mom started working for a naturopathic doctor who offered treatments for Betty's epilepsy at no cost to us. His offer was helpful because we were struggling financially and could not afford to get health insurance. I was first introduced to health insurance as a first-year undergraduate college student because it was mandatory.

On my first winter break from college, I was sharing Betty's room when the bed started violently shaking one night. Betty's rigid arms and legs thrashed uncontrollably as her entire body convulsed. I shook her, pinched her underarm, hoping she would "snap out of it." I had never witnessed anything like this. It lasted for what seemed like an infinite amount of time. When she recovered, she had no recollection of this episode. My admiration for her jovial lifestyle grew that night.

The seizures got progressively more frequent and worse. Without anti-epileptic medication, there wasn't much we could do. That summer, I decided we would spend more time together. When I returned home in May, I got free tickets to a Michelle Branch concert. Betty loved it! If only I knew our time together would be short-lived. During one of her grand mal seizures the morning of July 4th, 2003, at fourteen, Betty's heart stopped. That day, Betty gained her independence from the atrocious disease of epilepsy while we mourned to the sound of shooting fireworks.

My friend, sister, and confidant was gone. How could I possibly keep going forward through grief? Thankfully, GOD sent my best friend Derek in college to help me through the emotional paralysis grief was causing. After the initial year following her death, songwriting became another way to process the loss. Many of the lessons learned through this season today help me share the LORD's work with people who are grieving when the occasion arises. I marvel at how GOD can still draw creative productivity from what the enemy intends for evil.

Unfortunately, this would not be my only experience with familial grief. My youngest sibling and brother Frank Jr. lost his battle with mental illness in 2014. This often overlooked "cancerous" disease plagues many families and has recently risen to the forefront of public attention. Frank Jr. was an Eagle Scout, the life of the party, a hilarious comedian, a great friend, and a compassionate young man. He experienced the onset of this disease at the tender age of eighteen during his first semester of college. Having never experienced this before, our family, from October 2013 through July 15, 2014, tried everything we could to help him.

However, according to the law, the bottom line was that he was over eighteen and had to help himself. We were fighting as hard as we could, having already lost Betty to epilepsy. We did not want to lose Frank as well. On Tuesday, July 15th, 2014, Frank ended his life. I was devastated! If someone had told me this would happen a year before as we celebrated his graduation as the captain of Woodson High School's wrestling team, an upcoming Christopher Newport University student, and soon-to-be Eagle Scout, I would have dismissed them.

Hundreds of people attended Frank's memorial at the American Legion building in Fairfax City on July 27th, 2014. His Boy Scout Troop 1887, along with many dearly loved friends and family, witnessed the impact of Frank's beautiful life in a way my mom, Winnie, and I will remember forever. My most memorable moment from the memorial was when people sang "Blessed Be Your Name" by Matt Redman.

I felt like a hundred pounds were weighing on my chest until that moment. When they started, it was as if I could not breathe, but toward the middle of the song (for my musical peers, the bridge), I raised my arms in surrender. Suddenly, the weight was lifted, and my tears just flowed continuously. My friends later mentioned that it became a moment of worship. Pastor Fred, a family friend who facilitated the memorial, did an altar call, and that day some of the attendees gave their life to CHRIST.

The people who sang the song that day used their creativity in a way that powerfully ministered to me. Being the recipient of creative productivity in the midst of grief, I felt like a balm lathered my soul. Hearing that people accepted CHRIST restored my hope. This moment allowed me to grieve fully what had been a whirlwind of life-transforming events. I experienced what it meant to be the recipient of the GOD-led creativity.

No Regrets When Creative Productivity Takes Place

I would do almost anything to see Frank Jr. and Betty again here on earth. Yet, I would do nothing to change the productivity in expanding GOD's kingdom, which was a result of the creativity from many who helped facilitate their memorials.

In CHRIST, I have been both the recipient and participant in creative productivity. He strengthens me to keep going because of the authentic relationships forged in my life, starting with my relationship with Him. I know I am not traveling my journey alone. I realize no one should have to travel their journey alone, especially when every person is blessed with gifts and communication tools from the LORD and the creativity to use them effectively for His Kingdom.

I share these vulnerable parts of my life in this chapter to encourage you the reader, and others to always persevere in engaging in creative productivity, despite all obstacles as GOD leads. You never know whom you are impacting for the sake of His Glory.

Part II

HOW DO I START?

CHAPTER 8:

MEET YOUR FRENEMY - DISCIPLINE

Invite a Disciplined and Strategic Approach to Creativity

<u>Are Sustainable Practices in Place to Foster Creative Productivity?</u>

EARLIER THE CONCEPT OF HAVING multiple streams of productivity was presented. It is time to hone in on the key to handling multiple streams of creative productivity in a sustainable manner once GOD leads you: discipline.

Have you ever been in a situation where you started to design or improve a process, conceive an idea about something to engineer, solve a theorem, write a song or poem, generate a choreography, and could not stop? Have you ever pushed forward to the point where you did not stop to eat, or you chose to delay going to the bathroom because you were "so close to being done" only to find it would take another hour?

The excitement, joy, and desire to want to see the outcome of the project and its impact can be exciting and fulfilling. It is easy to get engrossed in the creative process when integrating creativity, especially once the fruit of the tools provided in this book becomes evident. I get it, trust me! However, I encourage you to use caution and creatively implement measures of discipline to foster and protect a wholesome life. In the absence of discipline, your creativity can become a tool for self-neglect and neglect of other critical factors of life (e.g., healthy relationships with friends and family).

In the absence of discipline, your creativity can become a tool for self-neglect and neglect of other critical factors of life (e.g., healthy relationships with friends and family).

We can glean healthy practices from the Biblical book of Genesis. GOD in the act of creating the universe took time to pause, reflect, and acknowledge that His day's creative productivity was good.[8] This example presents a potent litmus test for healthy creative productivity.

According to Genesis, on the seventh day GOD rested. He sets an example for how even with His might and power, though He did not need to pause, He chose to. As creative beings, we can choose to be the ones to apply creativity as GOD leads us or we can be consumed by being creative to the point where it becomes the idol that leads us, rather than GOD.

Refuse to let that family member or friend suffer because you are using creativity as an excuse instead of spending time with them. That is a blocker to true creative productivity. Prioritize GOD, family, Church, and wellness of mind, body, soul, spirit, and relationships. Balance and the application of discipline in applying GOD-Given creativity is the best fuel for powerful impact.

"Flag-on-the-Play" - Unhealthy Practices!

If elements in your life are starting to wither because of your engagement in creativity, it is time to creatively problem-solve. This could be symptomatic of a belief that your creativity is fleeting and won't be there in the same capacity if you take a break. The truth is that creativity is an ongoing and immovable part of who you are. Know that there is plenty more where that came from. In other words, you can take a pause and pick up where you left off. I promise that if you

---

8 "Genesis 1-2" (NIV), *Bible* Gateway, Accessed December 5, 2022, https://www.biblegateway.com/passage/?search=Genesis+1-2&version=NIV.

apply discipline to your creative projects, you will increase your creative productivity overall and grow in the security of knowing your creative gifts are not going anywhere.

Just because you're pausing in the creative outlet you prefer does not mean that there is no way to exert creativity elsewhere. When you return to what you were doing, you can pick up where you left off in a better way. Do you trust the LORD's leading to guide your creative process when you apply discipline?

05 - "Tis So Sweet to Trust in JESUS" –
Arrangement ©2022
A cappella vocals arrangement written and performed by
Emma Boa-Durgammah
Original Song by William J. Kirkpatrick (1882)
(Public Domain)
Recording by Monsell Carter

**Scan or visit
https://linktr.ee/creativityinus to hear this song**

VERSE 1

'Tis so sweet to trust in JESUS,
Just to take Him at His word;
Just to rest upon His promise;
And to know, thus saith the LORD.

CHORUS

JESUS, JESUS, how I trust Him,
How I've proved Him o'er and o'er,
JESUS, JESUS, Precious JESUS!
O for grace to trust Him more.

VERSE 2

O how sweet to trust in JESUS,
Just to trust His cleansing blood;
And in simple faith to plunge me,
Beneath the healing, cleansing flood.

CHORUS

JESUS, JESUS, how I trust Him,
How I've proved Him o'er and o'er, over and over again,
JESUS, JESUS, Precious JESUS!
O for grace to trust Him more.

CHORUS

JESUS, JESUS, how I trust Him,
How I've proved Him o'er and o'er, over and over again,
JESUS, JESUS, Precious JESUS!
O for grace to trust Him more.

VERSE 3

I'm so glad I learned to trust Thee,
Precious JESUS, Savior, Friend;
And I know that Thou art with me,
Wilt be with me to the end.

CHORUS

JESUS, JESUS, how I trust Him,
How I've proved Him o'er and o'er, over and over again,
JESUS, JESUS, Precious JESUS!
O for grace to trust You more.

CHORUS

JESUS, JESUS, how I trust Him,
How I've proved Him o'er and o'er
JESUS, JESUS, Precious JESUS!
O for grace to trust You more.
O for grace to trust You more.
And o for grace to trust You more.

Time to Make Room

⇨ Pray and make time to apply your GOD-Given creativity for at least ten minutes a day.

⇨ Learn to stop at exactly ten minutes.

    o Part of integration in your day-to-day is sustainability. It may not be sustainable for you to dedicate three hours every day to integrating creativity, given what is currently on your plate. However, it is better for you to have consistency and to practice the discipline of showing up for GOD and yourself. Integrate creativity in bits rather than doing it ad hoc and eventually abandoning it.

    o This exercise will also provide boundaries, so your creativity does not overtake you as a person or risk becoming an idol in your life.

CHAPTER 9:

WHAT'S IN YOUR TIME WALLET?

Create a Time Budget

<u>Time Is God's Gift to Humanity!</u>

TODAY, I INVITE YOU TO resist viewing time as a source of pressure going forward. It is a gift that keeps on giving when it is handled with care. The intent of this chapter is to encourage you amidst an ever-increasing fast world to practically examine your current use of time and

Time is a powerful gift if handled intentionally!

prayerfully take small consistent steps toward improving its efficiency.

This chapter is also meant to serve you by offering a practical tool that can help you begin a journey toward integrating creative productivity into your life. When Adam and Eve were tasked with naming and categorizing GOD's creation, they had access to everything GOD had to offer and could freely and productively be creative in this endeavor. Once they sinned and were separated from GOD, the work continued but was harder because their complete access to the Sovereign Creator of all and the Source of their creativity became limited.

This does not have to be the case for us by the Grace and Power that CHRIST offers if we accept to journey with Him. Time is one of the most potent gifts GOD gave us to practice stewardship of the creativity He entrusted to us.

Allocating time for creative productivity starts with four simple yet critical steps to take:

1. First and foremost, invite GOD to enter your heart if you have not already, and take over your life.
2. Foster your relationship with Him by spending time in prayer in the form of simple and frequent heartfelt conversations with Him — spoken words are not always necessary — just communicate with your heart.
3. Specifically, pray He will reveal the skills, gifts, and tools He gave you to serve Him and be creatively productive.
4. Obey as He leads.

As you do the above, I pray you find the tool within this chapter will help you identify where you can redirect your time or ideally get confirmation that you are already making adequate time to serve GOD with your gifts.

<u>Time Budget Tool</u>

There is a total of 168 hours in the week per GOD's grace, so let's start a template that allows us to spend it wisely and in a balanced way. A word of caution; the tool below is not meant to be used to add more pressure to your life or others' lives. If used properly, it should serve as a tool to:

1) Guide you and increase awareness
2) Encourage you to make gradual steps toward integrating time for tending to your relationship with GOD
3) Identify when to say no
4) Identify when to say yes
5) Allocate time for tending to the maintenance of you as His temple
6) Allocate time for family, and
7) Make time for creative productivity in your life

If you have been the driver on a busy highway, you can attest to the fact that there are more than enough factors already putting pressure on you daily. Therefore, there is no need for more pressure to occupy space on your plate. If you start self-condemning because the unexpected comes up that alters a few days or you are not perfectly adhering to this template, please put it aside, pray, recalibrate, then come back to it when ready. This tool is supposed to be a great step toward freedom, not something that leads you to place added pressure on yourself.

To start, write down two things you wish you had more time to do:

1) _____

2) _____

Next, replace or add to the "Activity Description" column below that I added as a baseline. Complete the amount of time you would like to allocate to each ensuring they add up to 168 hours in the week. Lastly, break down the time by day.

Weekly Budgeted Time

Activity Description	Time per Week	Time per Day	Notes
Time with GOD	-- Hours / Week	-- Minutes / Day	
Temple Care (self-care)	-- Hours / Week	-- Minutes / Day	
Family Time or Recharge Time	-- Hours / Week	-- Minutes / Day	
Ministry	-- Hours / Week	-- Minutes / Day	
Further Learning / Get informed about something new	-- Hours / Week	-- Minutes / Day	
Paid or Volunteer Vocational Work	-- Hours / Week	-- Minutes / Day	
Exercise	-- Hours / Week	-- Minutes / Day	
Meal Prep and Meal	-- Hours / Week	-- Minutes / Day	
Entertainment	-- Hours / Week	-- Minutes / Day	
Night Routine	-- Hours / Week	-- Minutes / Day	
Sleep	-- Hours / Week	-- Minutes / Day	
Unexpected Interruptions (Breathing Room)	-- Hours / Week	-- Minutes / Day	
Follow up with social network (e.g., friends)	-- Hours / Week	-- Minutes / Day	
Other	-- Hours / Week	-- Minutes / Day	

Once I created the time budget tool you just reviewed and completed it for myself, I quickly discovered that my budgeted time needed to be broken down so I could get clarity on my usual workday in contrast to my weekend day. This tool has been revelatory and allowed me to make shifts as needed. Therefore, the following tables are meant to be adjusted to reflect your average workday and your average weekend day. Note the difference between the weekdays and weekend days in the Activity Description columns for the tables below.

Average Weekday

Activity Description	Time per Week	Time per Day	Notes
Time with GOD	-- Hours / Week	-- Minutes / Day	
Temple Care (self-care)	-- Hours / Week	-- Minutes / Day	
Family Time or Recharge Time	-- Hours / Week	-- Minutes / Day	
Ministry	-- Hours / Week	-- Minutes / Day	
Further Learning / Get informed about something new	-- Hours / Week	-- Minutes / Day	
Paid or Volunteer Vocational Work	-- Hours / Week	-- Minutes / Day	
Exercise	-- Hours / Week	-- Minutes / Day	
Meal Prep and Meal	-- Hours / Week	-- Minutes / Day	
Follow up with social network (e.g., friends)	-- Hours / Week	-- Minutes / Day	
Entertainment	-- Hours / Week	-- Minutes / Day	
Night Routine	-- Hours / Week	-- Minutes / Day	
Sleep	-- Hours / Week	-- Minutes / Day	
Unexpected Interruptions (Breathing Room)	-- Hours / Week	-- Minutes / Day	
Other	-- Hours / Week	-- Minutes / Day	

In the following table, your biggest adjustment can be what replaces the vocational work slot from the average day.

I also recommend allotting more unplanned time at some point throughout the weekend.

Average Weekend Day

Activity Description	Time per Week	Time per Day	Notes
Time with GOD	-- Hours / Week	-- Minutes / Day	
Temple Care (self-care)	-- Hours / Week	-- Minutes / Day	
Family Time or Recharge Time	-- Hours / Week	-- Minutes / Day	
Ministry	-- Hours / Week	-- Minutes / Day	
Further Learning / Get informed about something new	-- Hours / Week	-- Minutes / Day	
Rest or Unplanned Time	-- Hours / Week	-- Minutes / Day	
Exercise	-- Hours / Week	-- Minutes / Day	
Meal Prep and Meal	-- Hours / Week	-- Minutes / Day	
Entertainment	-- Hours / Week	-- Minutes / Day	
Night Routine	-- Hours / Week	-- Minutes / Day	
Sleep	-- Hours / Week	-- Minutes / Day	
Unexpected Interruptions (Breathing Room)	-- Hours / Week	-- Minutes / Day	
Keep in touch with social circle (e.g., friends, distant relatives)	-- Hours / Week	-- Minutes / Day	
Other	-- Hours / Week	-- Minutes / Day	

<u>Next Steps</u>

Pray. I leave you with this prayer to end this chapter. LORD, GOD, Giver of time and the wisdom to spend time, I pray you will permeate every decision made around how to steward and spend the great gift You have given us in a way that is honoring to You and pleasing in Your sight. Take over, HOLY SPIRIT. Guide us according to Your will! Amen!

CHAPTER 10:

DON'T WORRY, JUST DO IT QUICKLY!

Overcoming Procrastination

Do the Difficult or Nonengaging Quickly!

DRAINING MUST-DOS ARE A PART OF life. These are activities that can be draining because they underutilize the creativity we have, either due to difficulty or not being engaging enough. An example of a draining must-do for me is folding clothes. It is not something that I enjoy. However, it is a necessary part of a functional person's life. It is a task for me that presents difficulty, not because it is complex, but rather because it is boring to me as a standalone task. For some of my friends, this is a therapeutic task. For me, watching the fire burn in a fireplace at night with all lights off as I sit in comfortable clothes to the sound of jazz for a couple of hours, is my version of therapeutic. Some of my friends would need to gamify this activity.

I recently talked to my best friend Derek about a situation that was bothering me. He listened, then offered a simple but transformative set of instructions. He said: "Breezy, you need to gamify this situation. Come up with a strategy and make a game out of this experience." These instructions were powerful because they taught me two invaluable lessons: 1) even if the weight of the difficulty seems draining, it is possible to view

"Breezy, you need to gamify this situation. Come up with a strategy and make a game out of this experience."

it as a game, so progress is not impeded, and 2) there is creative strategy involved in unraveling a situation methodically to derive a systematic solution. A simple approach to combatting the difficult and the nonengaging is to gamify it and do it quickly.

Practical Examples of Gamifying the Difficult or Nonengaging

A few years ago, I had an ah-ha moment that is tied to the principle of gamifying the difficult or non-engaging. I am aware that I can lean toward being a perfectionist about the outcomes of projects I undertake. This disposition can bleed into difficult or non-engaging tasks, such as folding clothes. It was cumbersome because I was applying the same amount of care and investment in the areas I creatively enjoyed and the ones I did not. This was causing analysis paralysis in the areas I did not enjoy. My shift in mindset was realizing those tasks just needed to get done, even if their outcomes were not up to par with my expectations. However, perfectionism was not the focus. Getting it done was!

The solution was to make a game out of it, develop a new strategy, and apply it to things I did not enjoy doing. I made it fun by deciding to only fold clothes to an engaging show, movie, or loud worship music. I made it quicker by buying hangers for 90% of my clothes to avoid having to fold every-thing. I made it even more fun by playing basketball with the clothes I had to fold, such as head scarves, once everything else was hung. This has done wonders as I now enjoy the game that comes along with "folding" clothes. It is no longer a standalone task for me. A similar approach can be applied to difficult things. Make a game of breaking it up into tiny morsels and creatively ideate and commit your brainstorm to writing until a solution becomes apparent.

For example, I remember not having enough to pay simple bills in my twenties. Through a series of circumstances, my small salary supported my brother, sister, mother, and me. This season of my life was, at best, difficult and at worst, dreadful, but by the grace of GOD, one He got me through. I made a game out of budgeting for the next week. When I was in the red, which was every month, I would see if I could be in the red a little bit less than the month before. I learned to celebrate the difference in dollars or pennies from one month to the next and treat myself to my favorite candy bar when victorious. Of course, the treat would only come if I was able to have a slight uptick in debt reduction from the previous month even after I purchased my candy bar. This seems small, but this little thing to look forward to at the end of the month was something that gamified a situation that was otherwise exhausting and emotionally draining.

Here is another practical example of a gamification model for the complex. I have noticed that the writing process is a bittersweet undertaking for me. I do not enjoy writing the first draft. I enjoy editing, but it takes time, so ultimately, that process stops being enjoyable. However, I find the ideating and creative process very fulfilling. Therefore, I decided to dictate my first draft to remove the stop-and-go of typing so I could freely ideate. Side note — a special thanks to Ben Johnson for this idea to dictate. Josh and Jamie, you have done a wonderful job raising your kids and impacting your community, including me!

I then took to the keyboard for edits. I have learned to gamify an otherwise treacherous process that taps into my past where certain experiences, which I will explain shortly, had falsely led me to believe I could never be a decent writer. Ultimately, writing about creative productivity so you and I can be impacted as GOD leads supersedes my fears from the past. It is worth me gamifying this process to get this work done.

If you have a story to tell but writing presents difficulty, there is hope! For context, I was a young immigrant to the United States who failed the Virginia literacy test twice before passing it in sixth grade. French is my first language, and English was not second nature despite having learned it briefly before age three. Therefore, it was difficult to put my thoughts into English for years. My father, at the time, believed it was important for our family to be fully immersed and asked that I watch two hours of television or listen to the radio to get up to speed as soon as possible with the English language. However, he would not allow my sister or me to take an English as a Second Language ("ESL") course. I would not recommend this approach to learning English because it was depressing and isolating at such a young age. There is wisdom to taking a structured ESL class and supplementing it with television and radio. However, I am grateful for some of the positive outcomes from that experience.

The shock of learning English that way turned me away from wanting to pursue any career that involved writing. I was a big fan of math because it involved little writing and I excelled at it. However, in eleventh grade, an English teacher of German descent taught me to look at an essay as a math equation where the thesis represented what came after the equal sign and the body paragraphs were the elements of the equation that needed to add up to whatever came after the equal sign. Her gamification of the difficult helped me realize and appreciate that writing had a structure. This concept powerfully resonated with me. Her gamification of the difficult inspired my efforts to write, which decades later is still producing fruit as I write this book today.

The Perfectionism Trap

The problem in seeking perfection, even in small tasks like folding clothes, was that I would get stuck and self-condemn for the time it took me to do the task. When gamification was applied, the time spent on perfectionism was redirected to enhancing the streams of productivity. This led to more enjoyment, and in CHRIST, fulfillment.

The reality is that perfectionism never matters because it is not attainable. It is perhaps the greatest enemy of creative productivity and a journey toward a FACE, a Fulfilled, Actionable, Creative Existence. Perfectionism is a byproduct of control. It is a desire to want to be exact in the execution of all projects. It undermines the variable nature of most projects, people, and life in general. Therefore, this tip of gamifying the difficult and nonengaging for everyone is of utmost importance so the important things can be addressed in a healthy manner.

For example, though my goal may be to exercise every morning, it is better to accomplish an 80% success rate, than to do nothing at all. The same goes for any creative project. At the expense of sounding controversial, something done at 80% quality is preferable to getting stuck and never doing anything at 0% action rate, despite a desired 100% quality outcome.

Gamification Time!

⇨ Pray.

⇨ Identify your difficult or nonengaging tasks or projects.

⇨ Find ways to insert fun elements into those roles. Example: give yourself thirty minutes to tackle it, then reward yourself with a three-minute walk.

⇨ Identify where there can be an end to the nonengaging roles.

⇨ If the situation is one you cannot exit, insert fun elements that will help you endure the tasks.

CHAPTER 11:

A WISE PERSON WEARS MULTIPLE HATS

Multi-Vocational Options that Transform Creativity into Action

Multi-Vocational Individuals in the Bible

WHAT DOES TENT-MAKING HAVE TO DO with creatively using rhetoric and logic to teach and pioneer? What does songwriting have to do with being a warrior and ruling a kingdom? Paul, the teacher/Church structure pioneer/tentmaker, and David the songwriter/king/warrior, offer great examples of multi-vocational individuals in the

Bible who applied creativity to impact others for GOD's kingdom. David did not come from a family of musicians nor was discipled by great worship leaders. Yet, he was the most prolific worship pastor in the Bible and wrote most of the recorded Psalms in the Old Testament. Similarly, Saul who became Paul, though he was similar to the person we know as Hitler today given his persecution of the Jews who followed JESUS at the time, after accepting CHRIST as his LORD and Savior, was on fire for the LORD and wrote most of the books in the New Testament. Either could have decided to silo their creativity and focus on one role over another. However, they valued the LORD, the Source of creativity, too much to disregard His leading. As a result, their multiple roles were what sustained creative productivity for GOD's Kingdom.

<u>The Multi-Vocational Option Explained</u>

The multi-vocational option is an important one to consider to integrate creative productivity in your daily endeavors. A multi-vocational individual holds multiple roles. Within the context of creative productivity, this option allows for multiple streams of productivity that can have various points of impact as the LORD leads. The multi-vocational option requires: 1) a clear understanding of calling, 2) a genuine embrace of the gifts the LORD

The multi-vocational option is an important one to consider to integrate creative productivity in your daily endeavors.

has entrusted unto you, 3) a desire to use them **all** for His Glory as He leads you, 4) resilience to persevere in the calling, even when progress is threatened, and expectations are shattered, and 5) obedience to allow the HOLY SPIRIT to lead you toward the Fulfilled Actionable, Creative Existence He has for you.

Practical Multi-Vocational Examples Today

A multi-vocational option can apply if you work full-time while choosing to engage in your preferred creative outlet simultaneously. A day job can provide you the ability to pay your bills while engaging in a creative outlet that is burgeoning. Here are a few examples, ensuring you always pray before engaging:

- Allocate time at a certain frequency (daily, every other day, or weekly) to build a multi-vocational ministry plan.
- Join an after-work dance group and participate as a dancer or choreographer.
- Start a prayer call, prayer walk, or prayer running group in your workplace or after work.
- Draw pictures of Biblical concepts (e.g., a fruit and two people to describe Genesis chapter 3) to teach your kids as you take care of them before or after work or as a full-time parent. (Thank you, Feben and Stephen!)

- Reach out to someone at a frequency you choose to check in and speak life into their endeavors-in-CHRIST after your workday
- Write a book to impart wisdom as the HOLY SPIRIT leads each day after work.
- Plan and implement Church ministry activities at a determined frequency.
- Allocate time in your week to write a play at a determined frequency.
- Allocate time in your week to encourage people to get healthier physically and in prayer while you build your fitness business.
- Pastor a Church while you work part-time, full-time, or are self-employed.
- Use social media to impart knowledge to others as the HOLY SPIRIT leads while you work in your day job.
- Build a business as the HOLY SPIRIT leads while you work your day job.

A byproduct is that creativity used within one context will bring mindfulness about using creativity in other contexts. In other words, creativity applied outside your workplace will inevitably help you apply creativity in your workplace, even if it's in smaller ways. Ultimately, you can experience the joy and fulfillment necessary to further progress in those spaces. From a CHRIST-centered perspective, this will enable you to spread the Gospel through your actions, passions, and gifts.

My Experience as a Multi-Vocational Individual

I will not lie and pretend that this is an easy path. As someone who has been multi-vocational since 2008, I can attest to the importance of courage, perseverance, drive, and determination when engaging on this journey. You will question yourself at times and even think you're crazy for wanting to do it. You may even face opposition from others who believe they have your best interest in mind. However, pray, take heart, and trust the process if CHRIST leads.

Despite the challenges, being multi-vocational has been an anchoring factor in my life and prevented me from dwelling on one failed element or another for too long. Candidly, I get impacted when things do not go as expected. However, by the Grace of GOD, I have been able to move forward regardless of how impacted I am within one space.

This has been true in the face of grief when I lost my sister and brother, in the face of anger at various situations, whether in ministry or corporate America, or personally in the disappointment of strained or failed relationships. I am so grateful to the LORD for He inspired methodical ways for me to infuse creativity in various aspects of my life. I stand amazed at His calculatedness. This lifestyle in CHRIST enables me to have drive and experience joy every day, even if one arena of my life is more painful than another.

Discover if the Multi-Vocational Option is for You

⇨ Pray for discernment about engaging in a multi-vocational pathway.

⇨ Pray for the courage to be multi-vocational and engage in creative productivity if that is the LORD's will for you.

⇨ Determine which roles to include in your multi-vocational framework.

⇨ Decide how to say no to things that do not align with your multi-vocational pathway.

⇨ Gather the tools you need to be multi-vocational gradually and build wisely.

CHAPTER 12:

GOT SKILLS?

Power Your GOD-Given Creativity

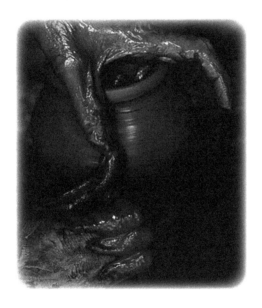

A Bronze Specialist and His Great FACE

THERE ONCE WAS A MAN WHO SPECIALIZED in bronze work named Huram.[9] The king of the land heard about his gift for transforming bronze into meaningful works

---

9 "1 Kings 7:13-47" (NIV), *Bible* Gateway, Accessed December 5, 2022, https://www.biblegateway.com/passage/?search=1+Kings+7%3A13-47&version=NIV.

of art and commissioned him to work on the furnishings of the Temple of the LORD. This king was known for his GOD-Given wisdom which he had requested from GOD prior to becoming king, though he had the option to request riches for himself. The king's name was Solomon and he reigned over Israel.

Solomon hiring Huram showed discernment because he believed the planning and the building of GOD's Temple required workers who strategically practiced faithfulness unto GOD, skills, and wisdom. The king was correct in his judgment because Huram over-delivered. The most notable testament to Huram's skill, wisdom, and understanding were the two pillars he built for the front of the Temple, which could be seen from far distances as people approached. He named the pillar to the south Jachin, which means the LORD establishes and the one to the north, Boaz, the LORD strengthens.[10] The Bible records Huram "was filled with wisdom, understanding, and knowledge to do all kinds of bronze work."[11]

There are few things that are more exhilarating to me than seeing someone exercise their skills in a way that is not just about the outcome of their work but rather a passion for GOD and the totality of the impact they will have through their work. What always fascinated me about this testimony in the Old Testament was that the pillars of the temple that were seen from miles away were designed by a man who

---

[10] "1 Kings 7:21" (NIV), *Bible* Gateway, Accessed December 5, 2022, https://www.biblegateway.com/passage/?search=1+Kings+7%3A21&version=NIV.

[11] "1 Kings 7:14" (NIV), *Bible* Gateway, Accessed December 5, 2022, https://www.biblegateway.com/passage/?search=1+Kings+7%3A14&version=NIV.

had the wisdom to handle the weight of the assignment — applying skills, tools and gifts under GOD's leading so creative productivity could be at work.

Use Your Skills and Gifts to Engage in Creative Productivity Every Day

GOD gave Huram the wisdom and understanding to worship Him and advance His Kingdom through actions within his vocation. What would it mean for us in our day-to-day to apply meaningful creative productivity to expand GOD's Kingdom in our vocations? What are the routine tasks we have excluded as being eligible for creative productivity? Is it possible there is a plethora of opportunities missed on a day-to-day basis that could be used for advancing the Kingdom of GOD? If you are not a believer in GOD, please note that the impact you have in making someone's day as they see your creativity at work is powerful. There is value in ensuring the creative existence GOD gifts to us is infused in every fabric of our day-to-day lives.

GOD gave Huram the wisdom and understanding to worship Him and advance His Kingdom through actions within his vocation.

CHAPTER 13:

IS THAT YOUR CRUTCH?

Education, Training, and Credentials Should be Tools, Not a Crutch

Organized Continued Learning Defined

THE DEFINITION OF ORGANIZED continued learning is education, training, or credentials from a subject matter expert, credentialing body, establishment, or educational institution that provides the knowledge and tools to operate in your gifts.

Who Is the Target Audience for this Chapter?

First, let me start by stating that this chapter specifically addresses post-secondary or continued learning through organized education. A kindergarten through twelfth-grade education is a must as a baseline. Engage in it, thrive in it, and fight against wasting it!

Is Organized Continued Learning a Prerequisite for Using Gifts?

The answer is a resounding NO! Why? This is the fastest way to impede your progress toward having impact for GOD. I cannot recount the number of times gifted individuals around me expressed GOD's leading and their desire to use their gifts followed by a statement about a lack of education, credentials, or training. I try to encourage them to start 1) praying and 2) at least researching for themselves first, especially considering the plethora of information available, so they can start using their gifts ASAP if GOD is leading them.

In tandem, I encourage them to pray about which organized continued learning path will best support their efforts. Organized education, training, or credentials should be a tool to further knowledge and the application of talent, not an excuse to delay its use. If you are waiting to use your gifts because you believe you need organized education, credentials, and training first, it has become your crutch.

To be clear, I am a big proponent of organized continued learning in its proper context. If it can powerfully further the use of your gifts, please proceed! It has played a phenomenal role in my journey to engage in creative productivity. Enjoy the equipping that comes from it. Resist the following motives and potential deterrents from a GOD-Led journey: grades, desire to brag about the degrees you have, number of acronyms after your name, the titles you get, or the people-pleasing you are engaging in toward parents, friends, or others. It is important to clarify roles. Titles help to do this in certain cases. The key is to never allow a role or title to define your identity.

With respect to grades, they are not bad as a byproduct but become toxic as an idol. The point is to check your motives and ensure the need for organized continued learning not an idol or obsession. You should be able to enjoy the passionate process of having organized education work for you.

I have been guilty of using continued learning through organized education as a crutch. I remember when I felt the LORD placed on my heart conducting seminars to encourage Christians to minister in their workplaces in 2012. My initial thought was to get more education in organizational development or event planning. My second thought was that I lacked resources such as a conference space or the finances to rent one. My limited view of a seminar was frankly the conferences I had attended or what I saw on TV. It wasn't until 2013 when by the Grace of GOD, I designed and ran my first one, and I was able to break it down into simpler necessities: content, place to meet, agenda, and people to attend. This simple exercise shifted my mindset about how accessible resources were.

Organized continued learning can be a powerful propeller toward successful creative productivity or a deadweight crutch that keeps you stagnant. You have the power to decide what it will become in your life. Organized continued learning for the sake of mere credentialing, validation, or perfectionism can be detrimental to the progress one must make toward unleashing GOD-Given creativity.

Discovering the Skills on Your Table

- Assess the skills you possess that do not seem conducive to using your creativity.
- Put on a consulting hat and discover connective tissues between your skills and gifts.
- Define three ways you can start integrating creativity in your day-to-day.
- Fight the urge to have organized continued learning as an idol or crutch!

Organized continued learning can be a powerful propeller toward successful creative productivity or a deadweight crutch that keeps you stagnant. You have the power to decide what it will become in your life.

CHAPTER 14:

REAL TALK – WHERE IS YOUR GETHSEMANE?

Identify Your Place of True Lament Before GOD

A Place to Keep It Real

HAVE YOU EVER BEEN FALSELY ACCUSED of something? Did you experience a situation where most people believed your accuser? You may have felt like no one could understand the weight of the accusation. JESUS in Gethsemane had a moment that far exceeds anything we could ever experience. He showed raw emotion and lamented over the weight of the task ahead: bearing the sins of humanity though He Himself was without sin. He expressed to the three apostles with Him "'My Soul is overwhelmed with sorrow to the point of death. Stay here and keep watch with Me.' Going a little farther, He fell with His Face to the ground and prayed, 'My Father, if it is possible, may this cup be taken from me. Yet not as I will, but as You will.'"[12] Gethsemane was a place where JESUS was real and raw in His lament, and fervently prayerful when begging GOD to relieve Him from having to experience the events ahead of Him.

Where Do You Productively Lament Broken Expectations?

Where is your place of true lament where you can mourn lost expectations in exchange for GOD's Expectations? Do you have a space where you can re-center and keep it real before the LORD so you can engage in events to come in a Kingdom-centric manner with wholesome resilience? Without a Gethsemane, a place to be vulnerable before GOD, you can risk masking unresolved issues that one day can paralyze the way you advance GOD's kingdom.

I remember seeing the movie *The Shack* based on the fiction book. In

> "
> *Where is your place of true lament where you can mourn lost expectations in exchange for GOD's Expectations?*
> "

---

[12] "Matthew 26:38-39" (NIV), *Bible* Gateway, Accessed December 5, 2022, https://www.biblegateway.com/passage/?search=Matthew+26%3A38-39&version=NIV.

the movie, there is a scene where the main character Mack visits a garden that for all intents and purposes looks like chaos, a seemingly unsurmountable work. Mack and the character Sarayu who is meant to depict some elements of the HOLY SPIRIT dig a hole in the garden and spend some time working on improving it. Toward the end of the movie what is planted in the middle of the garden is watered with drops of tears. A beautiful tree emerges, and a bird's eye view of the garden reveals the vibrant and ordered flowers and vegetation surrounding the tree and how beauty was birthed from pain. *The Shack* is where GOD performs spiritual heart surgery on Mack because it is the place where he lost his daughter and his heart hardened toward GOD.[13]

This was Mack's Gethsemane. Every tear Mack shed in the shack was used to water the trees planted in the garden of his heart. The process that took place in Mack's Gethsemane brought fruitfulness to his life journey. This place was where his lament was transformed into resilience.

I admit there are times when ministry and serving have taken precedence over prayer. I used to serve as part of a ministry that offered Bible study to juveniles in jail. Due to my work schedule, I was often rushing from my day job to the detention center. The difference was palpable when in my rush, I did not pray. I learned through serving the kids that they tend to be more receptive to the Gospel than those of us who are free because they have been involuntarily stilled for such a time as this. Therefore, I take very seriously the privilege of sharing the Word of GOD with them.

---

[13] William Young, *The Shack* (England: Hodder & Stoughton, 2008).

I recall one of the days I was serving. Since I was rushing from work that day, I asked to be a one-on-one counselor instead of teaching the group because I felt entirely depleted, and we always had someone to back us up if we could not teach. I did not want to be inauthentic in delivering the message to the children in attendance since I was still feeling rushed.

It worked out perfectly because in my one-on-one, we took some time to first pray. I was authentic with the teen and had the teen pray for me. Praying for me gave her a sense of empowerment to know she could minister unto others from exactly where she was with exactly what she had. That day she and I felt powerfully that where two or more are gathered, in that place, GOD is also, as per Matthew 18.[14] The Gethsemane experience can also take place on the go while commuting. It does not have to be like anyone else's. It just needs to exist somewhere in your life.

My Gethsemane is in the privacy of my home in complete darkness with a keyboard, singing and playing at times, or just sitting in silence to listen to Him between songs. It is in these moments of worship that milestone transformation has taken place in my life, where the messiness became consciously or unconsciously ordered, where tears flowed but felt collected to be used for His Glory. My Gethsemane is a place of authentic intimacy with CHRIST. I truly mean authentic.

It is the place where I've gone before the LORD and could only say "I have nothing to say or offer today but I know You have not given up on me." It is also the place where I've

---

[14] "Matthew 18:20" (NIV), *Bible* Gateway, Accessed December 5, 2022, https://www.biblegateway.com/passage/?search=Matthew+18%3A20&version=NIV.

celebrated Him continuously alongside laments. It has been a place where I have felt the sturdiness of His foundation as the Rock of all things constructed in me for His Glory. In a similar way, He is the foundational Rock for those who believe in Him and desires to be this for you if you do not yet believe in Him. I pray the arrangement of "My Hope Is Built on Nothing Less" hymn below encourages you in your Gethsemane moments.

06 - "My Hope is Built on Nothing Less"
Arrangement ©2022
Music and spoken word written and performed by Emma Boa-Durgammah
Original hymn by Edward Mote (1834) (Public Domain)
Recording by Monsell Carter

Scan or visit
https://linktr.ee/creativityinus to hear this song

VERSE 1 – HYMN

My hope is built on nothing less
Than JESUS' Blood and Righteousness
I dare not trust the sweetest frame
But wholly lean on JESUS' Name

CHORUS – HYMN

On CHRIST the Solid Rock I stand
All other ground is sinking sand
All other ground is sinking sand, sinking sand

POEM – STANZA 1

As deers that graze
Where the water lays
Through morning dew
And day's new rays
I stand amazed
With steady gaze
At the Son of Hope
Who set my sins ablaze

POEM – STANZA 2

When He said so
My soul arose
And I proclaimed
LORD JESUS' Name
They said 'Who, them in CHRIST, I doubt!'
But You said 'Yes them!
For My Grace abounds!'

CHORUS – HYMN
On CHRIST the Solid Rock, I stand
All other ground is sinking sand
All other ground is sinking sand

POEM – STANZA 3
You, GOD, are due honor, glory
You are due worship, humility
You are due praise that is endless
Your Love reigns, You are timeless
Your Love helps when we're helpless
Your Love lifts when we're hopeless
Your Love stills when restless
We give You thanks and nothing less

MELODIC INTERLUDE – ROCK OF AGES HYMN
Rock of ages clef for me
Let me hide myself in Thee

POEM – STANZA 4
You extended grace
Though we shunned Your Face
You endured, You chased
And all our sins were erased

VERSE 2 – HYMN
When You shall come with trumpet sound
Oh may we then in You be found
Dressed in Your righteousness alone
Faultless to stand before Your Throne

CHORUS
On CHRIST the Solid Rock I stand
All other ground is sinking sand
All other ground is sinking sand

CHORUS
On CHRIST the Solid Rock I stand
All other ground is sinking sand
All other ground is sinking sand

Where Is Your Gethsemane?

⇨ What do you consider your Gethsemane?
⇨ How do you experience GOD in your Gethsemane?
⇨ Record two powerful transformative moments that have taken place in your Gethsemane.
    o Use these moments as a tool for remembrance.

CHAPTER 15:

JESUS RESTED, SO SHOULD YOU!

The Importance of Rest and the Fine Art of Saying "No"

Ending a Marathonic Lifestyle

"INSTANT HUMAN, JUST ADD COFFEE!" This anonymous painting was propped against a tray and intended to be blatantly visible upon entering my kitchen in Virginia. The only variables in that statement were "Emma" and "Coffee". Some examples were "instant Emma, just add ministry", "instant Emma, just add less sleep", "instant Emma, just add not letting go until things are fixed". The fallacy of that type of rhythm was that it screamed of instant gratification though sustainability was in question.

> **"**
> *Hurry runs rampant today and stunts spiritual growth. How can we counter this epidemic and take steps toward ending a marathonic lifestyle in all areas of our lives?*
> **"**

In Psalm 46:10, the LORD through David instructs: "be still, and know that I am GOD. I will be exalted among the nations. I will be exalted in the earth."[15] GOD equates stillness in Him with knowing Who He is. Yet, hurry runs rampant today and stunts spiritual growth. How can we counter this epidemic and take steps toward ending a marathonic lifestyle in all areas of our life?

The Dangers of a Marathonic Lifestyle

In his book *Addicted to Hurry*, Kirk Byron Jones warns against the risks affiliated with a lifestyle where hurry becomes the norm. This lifestyle may create the false notion that we are getting closer to achieving what we are running toward. However, we can end up running "out of enthusiasm", "to get things done", "because the clock is running", "because there is too much to do", "to acquire prized possessions", " to catch up", "to avoid

---

15 "Psalm 46:10" (NIV), *Bible* Gateway, Accessed December 5, 2022, https://www.biblegateway.com/passage/?search=Psalm+46%3A10&version=NIV.

being late", "because of our jobs", "to remain in control", "for success", "to please people", "for the rush", "to be first", "to get our share", "because we do not know how to stop" and getting nowhere closer to GOD or His Will for our lives.[16]

<u>My Abrupt Stillness</u>

Chronic hurry came to a halt in my life in 2013 when the LORD allowed me to be physically stilled due to illness. This lasted through 2015. I recall attempting to slow down before 2013, including marking days that were off limits in my calendar. However, something always came up and I inevitably compromised. I felt like I did not know how to stop. However, waking up with a paralyzed upper body will promptly do an effective job of stopping someone in the middle of their rat race.

Two weeks before I woke up paralyzed, my sister-in-CHRIST, Jamie, informed me that I was on her heart and the LORD told her to tell me that if I did not slow down, He would slow me down. My response was in retrospect arrogant though direct: "If GOD told you, He will confirm with me during my one-on-one time with Him." Thanking people, then letting them know I will check in with GOD is a practice I try to employ when someone offers a prophetic word to avoid the potential of buying into false prophecy. However, in that instance, I was reacting because I did not like what she had to say. I have since learned to just say thank you and directly bring it to the LORD in prayer.

---

[16] Kirk Byron Jones, *Addicted to Hurry: Strategies for Slowing Down* (Pennsylvania: Judson Press, 2003). 20-29.

The conversation I had with Jamie flashed through my head the morning I woke up paralyzed. It took me four hours to unlock my body so I could move. This was the start of a journey that lasted months. I would awaken every morning paralyzed and in excruciating pain. I had to spend hours trying to unlock every muscle to be able to move. Months turned into a couple of years and many unfruitful doctors' visits. A couple weeks after I finally realized that GOD had been trying to get my attention far before this happened, I woke up one blessed morning in December 2015 and was no longer in pain.

Growth through Stillness

In Exodus 24:13, "Moses rose up with Joshua, his servant, and Moses went up onto GOD's Mountain." Later in verse 18, the reader learns "Moses was on the mountain forty days and forty nights."[17] I often wonder what Joshua did for forty days while GOD and Moses were meeting face-to-face. I believe the reader gets a glimpse of who Joshua became in Joshua 1:6-7: "Be strong and courageous; for you shall cause this people to inherit the land which I swore to their fathers to give them. Only be strong and very courageous."[18]

In the stillness of the mountain, I believe GOD spoke to Joshua and transformed him from a servant boy to a servant

---

[17] "Exodus 24:13" (NIV), *Bible* Gateway, Accessed December 5, 2022, https://www.biblegateway.com/passage/?search=Exodus+24%3A13&version=NIV.

[18] "Joshua 1:6-7" (NIV), *Bible* Gateway, Accessed December 5, 2022, https://www.biblegateway.com/passage/?search=Joshua+1%3A6-7&version=NIV.

warrior ready for one of the most important transitions for the people of Israel; the defeat of Jericho. When you and I look at our lives, are there moments of stillness where GOD can perform His heart work in us? The unfortunate answer at times is, not many. I am thankful GOD did not heal me immediately physically so that I could heal spiritually. I gleaned powerful lessons from this time of stillness. This boot camp in stillness still bears fruit today. The morning I wrote this chapter I had an opportunity to course-correct a missed opportunity for stillness.

It was a busy day. My clients had many active projects earlier in the morning. I did not get a chance to eat until later in the afternoon. As I was getting ready to step out to get my very late lunch, a call came for another project. I started to take it and decided to intentionally segment the time to grab a bite to eat and enjoy a few breaths of fresh air on the beautiful 74-degree day. The wonderful outcome was that there was no harm done. My client eventually received what they needed and did not feel slighted by the moments I chose to nourish my body. After all, I am accountable for taking care of the temple, the body, the LORD has entrusted to me as a gift when He gave me life. This is why I refer to self-care in this book as temple care.

The "I-am-an-adult" Mindset

I recall it was not until my early thirties that I really understood what I am coining as the "I-am-an-adult" mindset. The "I-am-an-adult" mindset is knowing there are consequences to decisions and owning up to mistakes, but not living under constant self-condemnation or fear of "getting-in-trouble" as if I was still a child. Many of us grow up in age, but not out of stages of fear we experienced as juveniles. I have noticed that some of us are still stuck in a self-condemning, "getting-in-trouble" and insecure mindset when we make decisions to rest, be still, or are unintentionally late due to unexpected occurrences.

This is by no means to excuse chronic negligent or tardy behavior. The I-am-an-adult mindset rather dispels the notion of exaggerated reactions in response to the unexpected or what is needed to take care of ourselves. The reality is these choices are necessary for our spiritual, physical, emotional, and intellectual survival. For me, savoring life more fully and listening more carefully is where I choose to start. What will be your choice today?

Avoid Temple Foreclosure

"What agreement is there between the temple of GOD and idols? For we are the temple of the living GOD. As GOD has said: "I will live with them and walk among them, and I will be their GOD, and they will be my people."[19] GOD desires to dwell in each of us and guide us to fulfill His purposes which are for the common good. Is there enough real estate in us for Him to be able to dwell? How we maintain our temple as believers in CHRIST is important. "In Luke 11:24-26, JESUS

---

[19] "2 Corinthians 6:16" (NIV), *Bible* Gateway, Accessed December 5, 2022, https://www.biblegateway.com/passage/?search=2+Corinthians+6%3A16&version=NIV.

explains that an impure spirit can return to a clean heart, (i.e., a clean temple), while additional toxic elements can create a worse condition than existed prior to the place being cleaned and put in order.[20] How does that occur unless the gates to the temple are left open? Our inner being is GOD's temple. A relationship with CHRIST where we submit the care of His dwelling place in us to Him will help us lock the gates to a clean abode and have the security and discernment of the HOLY SPIRIT to maintain it. The passage in Luke 11:24-26 reminds me of the danger behind a lack of proper rest in CHRIST.

Resting in CHRIST is supposed to be restorative and a way for the spirit, mind, body, and soul to get back into the intended order He has for us and be cleansed. However, if there is a lack of habitual integration of rest into our schedule, we are the equivalent of the unlocked temple inviting anything and everyone to enter. Note, the toxic spirit did not return alone. It came back with the busy-ness of his unrest, drama, and more like him to back him up.

A word of caution – the amount of time needed to rest varies per person and should be a prayerful exercise. Timed rest is also not the only factor in the replenishment of a person. A person may not dedicate whole weekends to resting but if they do so daily by getting the same amount of sleep and integrating a proper amount of time with GOD and temple care (self-care), it could accomplish the restorative work needed. The aim is to integrate time that replenishes into your

---

[20] "Luke 11:24-26" (NIV), *Bible* Gateway, Accessed December 5, 2022, https://www.biblegateway.com/passage/?search=Luke+11%3A24-26&version=NIV.

schedule so your temple does not begin to foreclose under the unnecessary weight of factors that steal and monopolize your time.

I pray the lyrics to the song I wrote to Monsell's instrumental beats at the end of this chapter encourage you to be a proactive steward of the earthly living GOD gifted to you. If the currency is the energy and vibrancy to do the Will of GOD and it is being traded in the market like money is today, we should be alarmed that markets are down, people are leery, and temples are at risk of going into foreclosure. However, take heart! GOD wants to make us whole for the sake of His Kingdom. Will we say yes?

<u>Creative Ideas to Rest</u>

Resting is admittedly something I struggle with to date. However, there are creative ways I have been integrating it that have been helpful, and I would like to share.

- ⇨ Enter time for yourself in your calendar (e.g., morning time with GOD and workouts).
- ⇨ In your work calendar, enter time for lunch and normal breaks if you can.
- ⇨ Enter time in your calendar for organizational or follow-up work. Don't dismiss the fact that they take time.
- ⇨ Honor your commitment to rest like you would any other commitment.

⇨ Ensure every day has dedicated non-stress time included, whether it's doing a few jumping jacks, making your favorite tea, watching your favorite show, or taking a nap. I appreciate and admire my auntie Suya because every day she ensures she fits in a power nap.

⇨ Put your phone on silent for some time every day.

<u>Next Steps – Suggestions to Start</u>

1. Schedule more moments of agenda-less silence each day to simply breathe, pray, meditate, and listen in prayer:
   a. This can include making time first thing after breakfast, so you have enough energy to stay awake.
2. Try not to interrupt when people are speaking and count to two before chiming in.
   a. This is admittedly a continuous struggle for me, but when I practice this, it helps measure the pace of the conversation, convey active listening, and ultimately affects its depth.
3. Let go sooner of things that seem toxic and consuming.

I now invite you to close your eyes and listen to the lyrics of the original song below.

07 - "Protect GOD's Temple" ©2022
Vocal music and lyrics written and performed by Emma
Boa-Durgammah
Instrumental beats composed by Monsell Carter
Recording by Monsell Carter

Scan or visit
https://linktr.ee/creativityinus to hear this song

INTRO
Warning, need rest!
Rest, stay blessed!
Warning!

CONTEXTUAL PRE-VERSE
(Yes, new creative element to songwriting)
Hear the noise of temples
Foreclosing in droves
Lacking the residual
Currency of old
Time and restoration
Through the Word foretold
Restful occasions
Ensure our temples won't fold

VERSE 1

Markets were down
Leery were the sounds
The cashflow was low
That's why the temple foreclosed
Resting was a dream
The inside was so clean
Doors unlocked caved in
That's why the temple foreclosed

CHORUS

Protect GOD's Temple
You need rest
Protect GOD's Temple
GOD knows best
Protect GOD's Temple
GOD knows best

VERSE 2

The pressure was high
Time with GOD was down
The cashflow was low
That's why the temple foreclosed
Success was royalty
The worshipped god was money
Doors unlocked caved in
That's why the temple foreclosed

PRE-CHORUS
In CHRIST, rest heals fully
His covering prevails
When the enemy unduly
Breaks in he will fail
His grip will never hold me
My heart will never foreclose

BRIDGE
Resting in CHRIST will be
Honoring faithfully
What He sacrificed to clean
In Him there is healing

BRIDGE
Resting in CHRIST will be
Honoring faithfully
What He sacrificed to clean
In Him there is healing

CHORUS
Protect GOD's Temple
You need rest
Protect GOD's Temple
GOD knows best
Protect GOD's Temple
You need rest
Protect GOD's Temple
GOD knows best
Protect GOD's Temple
GOD knows best

ENDING
Protect GOD's Temple
You need rest
Protect GOD's Temple
GOD knows best
Protect GOD's Temple
GOD knows best
"Be still and know He's GOD"[21]
He's GOD

---

[21] "Psalm 46:10" (NIV), *Bible* Gateway, Accessed December 5, 2022, https://www.biblegateway.com/passage/?search=Psalm+46%3A10&version=NIV.

CHAPTER 16:

EVANGELISM...REALLY... SKYDIVING?

Every Moment Can Become a Tool for Creative Productivity

THERE ARE MANY TOOLS AVAILABLE TO help convey the Gospel to those who have either not been exposed or do not believe in CHRIST. I honor the efforts that have been exerted by many who generated these tools. Some are more effective than others and if they have any impact in introducing people to a relationship with JESUS, I praise GOD! However, I have personally found that the best way for me to communicate the Gospel is through sharing my personal experiences, along with GOD's Word, as led by the HOLY SPIRIT. Honest communication that is not anchored in our own agenda, insecurity, or desire to control someone's life, but rather from a deep love for people and a desire for everyone to have freedom in CHRIST, can be powerful.

Creative Tools for Evangelism

"Have you ever been skydiving?" The young woman's face, which moments ago had expressed boredom and cynicism, lit up. I had begun my conversation with her using one of the tools for evangelism I had obtained from the leader of the ministry of which I was a part. I quickly realized she was tuning me out, so I prayed silently and asked GOD to lead me. The next thing that came out of my mouth was my question about skydiving. She told me that she had always wanted to skydive.

I took that opportunity to share my experience about seeing everything become two-dimensional and easily trackable from 11,000 feet in the air. This was an enlightening moment for me. I also shared I had gone skydiving as my first act of freedom when I got

I quickly realized she was tuning me out, so I prayed silently and asked GOD to lead me. The next thing that came out of my mouth was my question about skydiving.

to college without telling my mom until I safely landed. She laughed and at that moment a powerful connecting point started to happen. Her face became inquisitive. She asked me about how my mom reacted. I shared she was mad that I did not take her with me. The young woman laughed some more. She asked what I meant by my enlightening experience. I asked what her choice would make if she had to pick between getting directions from someone with a bird's eye view or someone next to her who had never taken the route. She responded she would pick the person with the bird's eye view.

Perceiving GOD Moments that Can Be Creatively Communicated

I shared with her that for me, skydiving helped sharpen my perspective on problems we deal with daily. When I was up in the air at 11,000 feet it was evident that the largest, most multi-layered real-life issue we face as human beings is nothing but a two-dimensional problem to GOD. From the sky, I could clearly see how to get from point A to B because of my overall view from the plane.

She responded with a personal situation she was dealing with that made her doubt GOD is real and we talked through it. We prayed together and she said she would think about everything we discussed. She thanked me for taking the time to listen, talk, and pray with her.

Some may consider that encounter a failure because she did not accept CHRIST that day. This would be trivializing the power of the LORD's work through the conversation.

He enabled me to connect with another sister and share the Gospel. There is no way for me to know someone's heart. That is the reason it is of utmost importance that we consult with the HOLY SPIRIT before engaging and speaking to someone about JESUS.

Creative productivity was at work as a byproduct of my prayer that day. Our conversation was not something I had planned. Answering her question about skydiving or getting from A to B was not planned. However, GOD was allowing me to use a seemingly unrelated experience to profess Him, and His ability to maneuver our lives for the sake of His Glory.

There are life experiences you have had in the past or are going through that seem unnecessary but can one day become exactly what GOD uses to transform another person's heart. You have many purposes in this world. I encourage you to actively share your personal experiences.

Prayer for the Spread of the Gospel through Life Experiences

LORD, I pray You help us discern the ways You would like to spread Your Good News in and through us. Amen!

Part III

LEADERSHIP, MINISTRY, and
CREATIVE PRODUCTIVITY

CHAPTER 17:

INCOMING MAIL

Dear Leaders

FROM: MY HEART
TO: YOURS

HELLO JOHN AND JANE DOE, WHEN YOU stepped into leadership you were excited about helping others, especially because it meant serving CHRIST in the process. As you engaged in this process you realized that every individual has a different level of dedication and the quality of what they choose to present publicly may vary. You either consciously or unconsciously compare the output of others against what you would ever present, disregarding the fact you may be a perfectionist or in need of leadership, organization, planning, delegation, and/or communication skills to better motivate people who work for and with you.

This process has been frustrating if you want to be candid, and you have a hard time reconciling people's desire to work and serve CHRIST against their lack of commitment to improve the tools they possess, knowing dedication can enable them to better work to serve CHRIST. You are starting to get discouraged because the team's progress is slow or not visible. Can you relate? This is where I would like to pause.

Excellence for CHRIST vs. Our Perfectionism

Most likely, if you're leading in some way or another, you will relate to this chapter. I will be addressing this chapter from the perspective of someone who has been a part of praise and worship music arts as a Worship Leader, Band Director, Worship Advisor, Band and Choir Member, and helped numerous people use their gifts for the Kingdom of GOD. I have learned that every moment as a leader in this space is a platform for you to reflect CHRIST, even during rehearsals. Some examples of praise and worship platform arts leaders are worship team leaders, worship band leaders, Church or ministry choir directors, ministry musicians, praise dancers, mime dancers, fine arts presenters that convey the Gospel, modern dancers for CHRIST, and flag dancers, among many others.

Please see if you can relate to any of the following. You have had an opportunity to grow in your craft or skillset independently before you were called, volunteered, or "vol-un-told" to lead. The lessons that you learned while getting better in your craft have been invaluable and made you who you are. There is an adage that it takes 10,000 hours to perfect a skill. Perhaps you have even spent that much time on your art, whether at work or in ministry. For all intents and purposes, you recognize that it has been hard work. There may be a level of Godly giftedness that you have had an opportunity to exercise and, in doing so, have learned to expect excellence in anything, including what you publicly present. You may have even struggled with presenting anything until it was up to the standards you deem acceptable, which most likely are nothing shy of perfect. This alone can be frustrating.

If you add this to any skills gap in leadership, such as communication, organization, planning, and/or delegation, it can feel hopeless. However, take heart and put into action a plan to assess those skills gaps. First, when things go wrong, pray and ask GOD to reveal what you could have done better first before examining how others contributed. Conduct a survey with people you have had a hard time working with or leading. Separately, conduct another survey with those with whom you have enjoyed working. Prayerfully consider the feedback you receive. Resolve to lead better as you consider the remainder of this chapter.

What Was the LORD Thinking?

CHRIST, when sacrificing and resurrecting for us, gave humanity the option to invite Him into our hearts and accept His HOLY SPIRIT so we could be guided through life, especially when it comes to using our gifts for His glory. He understood there was no way we could ever execute to the level of perfection He could. Why would He ever choose to take the risk of potentially using our gifts in a clumsy way though He is an incredible and perfectly creative GOD? Even in asking Adam to name the birds of the sea and creatures

He had created, He knew that Adam could never do a better job than He could.

Yet, the LORD of the universe freely assigned this highly strategic and creative project of naming and stratifying everything He had created to someone whom He knew would not measure up to His output. Could it be that GOD is more focused on progress and process than outcome? Could it be that this is the reason He has patience with us in this very moment where we fall short? This is a powerful reason to extend grace as leaders.

If CHRIST did it, and we seek to follow Him, why would we not share His heart to see others progress, hopefully beyond anything we could ever do? Furthermore, it is most likely that others can do things better than we can if given the proper tools, training, prayer backing, and love they need to develop. As a leader, including those in praise and worship platform arts, you are signing up to represent the heart of CHRIST to those with whom you work and interact. There is a fundamental difference between expecting growth toward excellence for CHRIST and superimposing our perfectionism and/or projecting your skills gaps on people.

As a leader, including those leading from praise and worship arts platforms, you are signing up to represent the heart of CHRIST to those who are working with you

I confess I have been guilty of that in the past and admittedly, at times, still struggle. The saving grace is that

I am grateful for a daily relationship with GOD where He course-corrects me along the way, directly or through others. Since this is, for most of us, an arena where much effort, grace, and understanding of GOD and self has taken place, I am learning increasingly appreciate the progress and process it takes for someone to redirect their gifts toward serving GOD.

<u>Appreciation and Celebration</u>

As I appreciate and celebrate the progress and process in others and myself, I am able to let go of the expectation of a perfect outcome. A miraculous and fulfilling privilege occurs. I revel in the joy of being a fly on the wall to the progress and process GOD enables in others through me when He chooses. Most importantly, I get to witness people's hearts transform and get deeper in love with GOD because they are further using their gifts for the sake of His Kingdom. An added benefit is when outcomes far exceed my expectations.

When I was focused on the perfectionism of the outcomes, I missed that the spread of the Gospel was taking place right in front of my face. GOD was calling me to pause and like He did each end-of-day of creation, appreciate what was good. An interesting byproduct of this heart posture has been that people tend to output more quality work when they experience a leader who centrally cares about their relationship with CHRIST and how they use their gifts, not their own agenda or ego.

Encourage Improvement of People's Gifts in a CHRIST-Centered Way

This is not a dismissal about encouraging people to commit to practicing their GOD-Given craft and put in the effort. However, GOD cared enough about the process and progress to work with you and me and we ought to care enough about the process and progress of others and how He is working with them. We ought to celebrate even the small victories regardless of how they compare with our sense of what should be perfect. We ought to engage in lifestyle and when led, speak the Gospel, especially when we lead praise and worship platform arts.

From a practical standpoint that means that people's experience of you needs to be a combination of the heart of CHRIST, the grace of CHRIST, the truth of CHRIST, and the joy of CHRIST. When you are in a green room before presenting your art in front of people, are the conversations self-centered or so art-centric that those who are visitors or less familiar cower in silence and feel ostracized? I cannot express the number of times that has been the case where worship teams I collaborated with would barely say hello when they were getting "in the zone" before going on stage. This is a missed opportunity to live a lifestyle Gospel!

The sense of being a diva or the painfully and unreasonably yelling leader ought not to exist in a CHRIST-Filled environment. It is okay to ask for commitment, push people to work hard or discuss plans of action to improve their gifts. However, it is not okay to treat people as if you are better than them or mock them when they cannot deliver outputs you do not deem up to par. It is not okay to be so worried about how you are going to sound or perform that you cannot engage in a simple conversation with someone.

On the flip side, it is not okay to lie to people about the places of improvement that are needed. It is not okay to encourage a false path when the calling on their lives is clearly in another direction. Speaking in grace, spirit, and truth is much needed in this space as well. My prayer is that we will be agents of creative productivity and with CHRIST-like hearts and will focus on redirecting people to Him in everything they do, including the arts in which we partake.

Next Steps:

1. What are three missed opportunities for lifestyle Gospel you have experienced or unintentionally initiated?
2. What are three top ways you can improve as a leader?
3. What are your reasons for wanting to be a leader?
   a. A word of caution, if validation, legacy, or recognition are your reasons, they are fleeting and an opening for you to quit when expectations are unmet.
4. Who are two people the LORD is calling you to journey alongside and help grow for His Kingdom?
5. What are the top three ways you lean toward perfectionism as a leader?
6. What are the top three ways you lean toward excellence for CHRIST as a leader?
7. List three things you believe the HOLY SPIRIT is leading you to do in this arena.

CHAPTER 18:

TAG, YOU'RE IT!

Becoming a Responsible Leader

The Importance of Encouragers of Creative Productivity!

THANK YOU IF YOU ARE AN ENCOURAGER of creative productivity! Your contribution to the livelihood of those with whom you interact is invaluable! My music teacher Ms. Sylvia Taylor recognized the gift of music the LORD gave me when I attended her class in sixth grade. She encouraged me to go forward in honing that gift. In seventh grade, my music teacher, Ms. Brady asked me to teach one of my songs to the choir so they would sing an original piece that I had written entitled "People Gotta Care". These were small ways in which room was made for me to use the gift the LORD gave me through leaders who took seriously the responsibility of fostering the gifts they perceived in people. What I later discovered in forging a friendship with Ms. Taylor is that every morning she would pray over her classroom and students. I firmly believe GOD guided her decisions in navigating the elementary kids' hearts she needed to impact. Ms. Taylor exemplified creative productivity as a teacher without saying a word.

Go Forth and Make Disciples of Nations

Your desire to further creative productivity, whether a formal role has been ascribed to you or not, makes you a leader, a thought leader, and an advancer if you are willing to assume your responsibilities. JESUS in the New Testament brilliantly leveraged His apostles' skills, such as Simon Peter's talent for fishing, and journeyed with them to set the example. He taught them to use their readily accessible skills, tools, and gifts for GOD's Kingdom. He taught them they could live a fulfilled, actionable creative existence using exactly what they already had. He made disciples of nations by addressing their skills, tools, and gifts in addition to their hearts and faith.

<u>Ensure You Have the Right Motives</u>

Please allow me to address the elephant in the room if you consider yourself a leader in furthering creative productivity. Why do you truly want to do this? Are there any motives that are based on your desire to be credentialed, seen, validated, or appreciated? If so, I urge caution because these are not sustainable reasons to engage in being a thought leader or an advancer of creative productivity. Now is a good time to anchor your motives into proper context: GOD and His leading.

If one uses creativity to advance His Kingdom and creative productivity is the outcome sought, it is incumbent upon that person, especially if they want to engage in a leadership role, to creatively foster intimacy with GOD. As a byproduct, He will help you impact and inspire others for the sake of His Kingdom. Are you willing to help people discover that the LORD is the Source of all creative productivity for His Kingdom, not all creative outcomes? In doing so, He will reveal daily how to navigate spaces, peoples' hearts, and outcomes for the sake of His Glory.

Our posture as leaders in advancing creative productivity is to ensure we remain willing to serve rather than be served.

As creative leaders, our responsibility is to ensure that people are redirected to CHRIST and serve Him with their skills, tools, and gifts. We can be the reflective image of GOD through our actions under His Leadership and

Authority. Our posture as leaders in advancing creative productivity is to ensure we remain willing to serve rather than be served. This posture of service is elating and, in turn, becomes a great journey of FACE.

I pray every single person gets to experience what it means to be a servant leader that encourages and makes room for others to engage in creative productivity.

CHAPTER 19:

THE CLOCK IS TICKING!

How the Church Can Handle Present and Future Challenges

The Need for CHRIST in the Local Community

A CHURCH OR MINISTRY'S MISSION, under the leadership of the HOLY SPIRIT, can powerfully address the extent to which the local community believes it needs JESUS, its pain points, cultural dynamics, and socioeconomic considerations, among others. GOD has given the Church creativity to stay ahead and effectively handle the challenges of the present and future times. The need for JESUS is defined by how much the community is aware of and embraces Him. The material needs of the community are the gaps that are typically symptomatic of a need for JESUS. GOD-Given creativity under the leadership of the HOLY SPIRIT can play a critical part in consultatively assessing and then addressing the need for JESUS.

GOD has given the Church creativity to stay ahead and effectively handle the challenges of the present and future times to come.

For example, if hunger is pervasive in a community, assessing the community's needs results in feeding those who are hungry. However, assessing the need for JESUS should result in feeding the need for hunger while digging into the cause of hunger and discovering spiritual deserts that are fueling physical famines. An evaluative shift from "how do we win this community to CHRIST" to first "to what extent does the community believe it needs CHRIST" then "CHRIST, how do You want to make yourself known in this community through us as a ministry" can enable impactful and strategic initiatives.

John describes how Nathanael was invited by Philip to come and see JESUS of Nazareth who had been referenced by the Law of Moses and prophets. Nathanael in a snarky manner questioned if any good could come from a man from Nazareth. Instead of debating, looking down on Nathanael, or talking to others about his doubt, Philip invited him to come and see JESUS for himself.[22] Philip wisely discerned that Nathanael did not think he needed JESUS and was undermining His legitimacy. Philip had the wisdom to redirect Nathanael straight to JESUS. What happened next was remarkable:

"When JESUS saw Nathanael approaching, he said of him, 'Here truly is an Israelite in whom there is no deceit.' 'How do You know me?' Nathanael asked. JESUS answered, 'I saw you while you were still under the fig tree before Philip called you.' Then Nathanael declared, 'Rabbi, You are the Son of GOD; You are the King of Israel.'"[23]

I am glad Philip did not try to address Nathanael's criticism of JESUS on his own. He could have easily assumed Nathanael was perhaps not a good person to be a disciple of JESUS and dismissed him. However, JESUS knew exactly what Nathanael needed to come to the realization that he needed JESUS more than anything. Nathanael went to become one of the disciples of JESUS and found purpose in Him that day.

Today, JESUS knows exactly what the community around you needs, including those who may be thinking 'what good can come out of anything having to do with JESUS, the Church, or ministry?' To be honest, some of our deplorable actions as the Body of CHRIST merit this criticism because we took matters into our own hands instead of following His leading

---

[22] "John 1:44-46" (NIV), *Bible* Gateway, Accessed December 5, 2022, https://www.biblegateway.com/passage/?search=John+1%3A44-46&version=NIV.

[23] "John 1:47-49" (NIV), *Bible* Gateway, Accessed December 5, 2022, https://www.biblegateway.com/passage/?search=John+1%3A47-49&version=NIV.

and handling things with His spirit and character. Therefore, how can churches and ministries effectively redirect people to Him and have a Kingdom impact?

The following two questions are a simple starting point for getting a pulse on the local community's need for CHRIST:

1. What are the top three thoughts that come to mind when members of the community hear the following words: 'The LORD JESUS CHRIST'?
2. What are the top three genres of music that best speak to them?

Answers to the two questions above from as many people as possible in your local community will provide an authentic overview of the gaps in how people perceive CHRIST. This assessment will also help inform how praise and worship music that is CHRIST-centric can address the need for JESUS as led by the HOLY SPIRIT. In doing so, please do not forego having multiple touchpoints for people to experience GOD through music by adding variety to the genres of music you use to serve Him and people.

CHAPTER 20:

WARNING!

Burnout Jeopardizes Creativity

IF YOU ARE A SERVING MEMBER OF A CHURCH

or ministry, including those in leadership, your impact on the people GOD has entrusted in your life and on your local community is intricately intertwined with 1) the health of your relationship with GOD and 2) how you care for the temple He has gifted you, your health, and your well-being. JESUS said: "'Love the LORD your

> **"**
>
> Love of GOD
> + Love of Who
> We Are in GOD
> = GOD-Led
> Love of Others
>
> **"**

GOD with all your heart and with all your soul and with all your mind.' This is the first and greatest commandment. And the second is like it: 'Love your neighbor as yourself.'"[24]

The tool below is meant to help you conduct an analysis of where you stand and identify any impending dangers to the two core tenets of loving and serving others as CHRIST's hands and feet. The resources referenced in the footnotes are wonderful. I recommend reading them if you want to dig further.

Spiritual SWOT Analysis Tool

1. Strength — Do I have a support network independent of my ministry context that is invited to partner, dissent, lead, and correct me into the best person I can be in life for the ministries I serve?
   a. Sondra Wheeler presents wise insights that "relationships where ministers are not 'the Pastor' or viewed as leaders, are essential if ministers are to safeguard all the relationships in which they are, where they must be ever aware of the office they hold and the special responsibilities it brings."[25]
2. Strength — Do I have processes in place to assess and use the gifts and resources GOD provided for me to serve Him?

---

[24] "Matthew 22:37-39" (NIV), *Bible* Gateway, Accessed December 5, 2022, https://www.biblegateway.com/passage/?search=Matthew+22%3A37-39&version=NIV.

[25] Sondra Wheeler, *Sustaining Ministry* (Michigan: Baker Publishing Group, 2017), 52.

    a. How can I be GOD's hands and feet toward my personal and work connections, through my behavior and lifestyle, in my outlook on life.[26]

3. Weakness — Do I have a system in place to identify what Wheeler describes as 'danger signals' for ministers? These signals can lead to spiritual and moral compromise.

    a. Clues that danger could be lurking: giving too much attention to appearance; becoming mentally preoccupied; altering, extending, or increasing the frequency of meeting times; seeking one-on-one interaction; offering inappropriate personal disclosures; preferring another's company; changing the kind or frequency of touch; not wanting contact with congregants to be viewed by others; deceiving one's partners or spiritual guide, among others.[27]

4. Opportunity — Has GOD called me to be a leader where I am positioned or aiming to lead even if it means having to do so without being assigned by someone in leadership?

5. Opportunity — Am I actively praying about my successor and presenting opportunities for them to grow in the ministry?

6. Opportunity — Do I best identify as a mission-maintenance team member or a transformation team member?

[26] Gil Rendle, Quietly Courageous (Maryland: Rowman & Littlefield, 2019), 77.

[27] Sondra Wheeler, Sustaining Ministry (Michigan: Baker Publishing Group, 2017), 98-110.

a. The mission-maintenance group is committed to preserving the core tenets of the mission of the church, culture, venue, and successful implementation plans through which church initiatives are carried out. An example of this could be a board of directors. This mission-maintenance team also provides cover for the transformation team because they care for the needs of the church and the local community while the transformation team forges ahead ensuring the church is missional in an adaptive environment where there is a need for rapid change. This will ultimately be the group that will choose to institutionalize changes brought forth by the transformation team.[28]

b. The transformation team will be the group that leads the efforts to innovate so the church can persist through changing times. Members of this group must be a combination of church staff and lay leaders who are cohesive and communicative. They can exert creativity, energy, credibility, personal maturity, and unwavering determination even in the face of pushback. They are resolute and enthusiastic about the ideas that will make a mission-oriented impact on the community for CHRIST. They can employ relational capital to generate genuine cultural change. They are a group willing to volunteer their time and disband once the ideas are adopted by the church and institutionalized by

---

[28] Tod Bolsinger, *Canoeing the Mountains* (Illinois: InterVarsity Press, 2015), 165.

the mission-maintenance team.[29] It is important to note that this team should be willing to let go once the assignment is complete.

7. Threat — Do I have a system in place to periodically assess what Tod Bolsinger describes as "six necessary relationships for leading into the unknown":

   a. Allies – people aligned with achieving the shared missions in which I am vested

   b. Confidants – people who have my best interest in mind first

   c. Opponents – people who disagree with the ways I approach achieving the shared mission

   d. Senior authorities – people who have been given authority to lead me and others

   e. Casualties – people who are no longer in touch with me and are relational casualties in my life. I pray GOD restores those even if it is apart from each another.

   f. Dissenters – people who disagree with me?[30]

8. Threat — Am I feeling threatened by any ministry initiative or anyone in the ministry, or Church, and if so, why?

---

[29] Tod Bolsinger, *Canoeing the Mountains* (Illinois: InterVarsity Press, 2015), 165.

[30] Tod Bolsinger, *Canoeing the Mountains* (Illinois: InterVarsity Press, 2015, 157 – 164.

Next Steps

My prayer for you and your ministries is that you will adopt an informed process to serving GOD and people. More intentionality will bode better results. GOD has gifted you with the ability to have incredible reach as ministries first spiritually, the quantitatively, and as He leads. I pray the tools above help you to engage in His work.

CHAPTER 21:

KINDLY RSVP

Your Invitation to a Creatively Productive Lifestyle

YOU ARE INVITED!

<u>Thank You and Word of Caution</u>

DEAR READER, THANK YOU FOR MAKING it to the end of this book. My sincere hope is that you will be energized to engage all the creative gifts the LORD has entrusted unto you for His glory. My encouragement is not to let anyone discourage you from engaging in those gifts. Use the tool I generated for you at the end of the book, and stay the course!

As a parting word, I pray that you examine the gifts you were blessed with and let go of any efforts to obtain or match the gifts you envy in other people. Envy and comparison can be the fastest route to the enemy's attempt to murder what GOD birthed in you. Envy and comparison prevent us from promptly activating and engaging in our gifts. The way forward is too bright to waste your time with these traps.

Seeds of Creativity in Us

As a starting point, think and pray about any seeds to spark the creativity in you that GOD may have been planting within your life all along. I remember when I was in an all-girls religious school at the age of seven in a French-speaking country. Mass was part of our scheduled events each day. I, unfortunately, was not really interested in anything GOD-related at that age, but my parents had me attend this school because the education was good. During a couple of the mass services, we sang a song that captured my ear. I really liked the melody and enjoyed arranging it real-time in my head. Fast forward to ten years after journeying with CHRIST. I tried to remember the song and could not because 1) the lyrics were in French when I first heard it and 2) I did not care enough to want to memorize the lyrics at the time.

Fast forward to thirty years after hearing the song, my sister-in-CHRIST Kristina suggested "Of the Father's Love Begotten" as a hymn that could be great for us to arrange for our Christmas program. I told her I was not familiar with the song. As soon as she started playing and singing it, I got chills. This seed was planted thirty years prior to that moment. Words cannot describe how grateful I was for the LORD's calculatedness when we sang an arrangement of this song for our Christmas program. I could see the creativity He had planted in me at work because it was now under submission to Him. GOD had been planting seeds all along, even before I had accepted Him as Savior. Wow! I am including an arrangement of this song, specifically for you, the reader, at the end of this chapter.

If you are willing to anchor in CHRIST and use your gifts for His glory, as a follower of His character, He will give you the steps needed to live a fulfilled, actionable creative existence.[31] Will you accept His invitation and engage in the creative productivity He intended for you?

---

[31] "John 10:10" (NIV), *Bible* Gateway, Accessed December 5, 2022, https://www.bible-gateway.com/passage/?search=John+10%3A10&version=NIV.

08 - "Of the Father's Love Begotten" – Arrangement ©2022
Musical arrangement written and performed
by Emma Boa-Durgammah
Original song by Aurelius Prudentius, translated by
John Mason Neale, Henry W. Baker, Roby Furley Davis
(1582) (Public Domain)
Recording by Monsell Carter

Scan or visit
https://linktr.ee/creativityinus to hear this song

Of the FATHER's Love begotten
Ere the world began to be,
He is Alpha and Omega,
He the source, the ending He,
Of the things that are, that have been,
And that future years shall see,
Evermore and evermore

Let the heights of heaven adore Him
Angels hosts, His praises sing
Powers, dominions bow before Him
And extol our GOD and King

Let no tongue on earth be silent
Every voice in concert ring
Evermore, evermore

CHRIST, to Thee with GOD the FATHER
And O HOLY GHOST, to Thee
Hymn and chant and high thanksgiving
And unwearied praises be
Honor, glory and dominion
And eternal victory
Evermore and evermore

ENDING
Honor, glory and dominion
And eternal victory
Evermore and evermore

Appendix

Time to Strategize!
Your Creative Productivity Playbook

Your Potential for Creative Productivity

THE BEGINNING OF YOUR CREATIVITY occurred when the LORD included it in the fabric of your being as He was making you in His image. In Genesis 2:19, He provided the resources for humanity to be creative. The best, most fulfilling outcome to using the gifts He has entrusted to you is to offer them as worship unto GOD and productively impact others for the sake of His Kingdom. This is creative productivity. You are invited to use this quick tool as a starting point.

WHERE IS YOUR CREATIVITY USED?

Baseline Concepts from this Book

1. What does FACE stand for?
2. What is the definition of creative productivity?

Relationship with the Source of Creativity

1. Accept the invitation to a life with CHRIST, who is the Source of a fulfilled, actionable creative existence.
2. Invite Him to take over your gifts and give you discernment on how to best use them.

Where Are You Positioned?

1. List three environments where you already have roles that use your creative gifts. Remember to list unconventional spaces where creativity is not often referenced. See chapter 5.

_____

_____

2. What makes it easy to use creativity in those environments?

_____

_____

3. List three spaces you are in that do not leverage your creative gifts. Remember unconventional spaces where creativity is not often referenced. See chapter 5.

_____

_____

4. What prevents you from using creativity in those environments?

_____

_____

You're invited to Explore Further

I would like to invite you to a deeper journey and more practical tools. How? Visit https://linktr.ee/creativityinus.

Lastly, I would love to hear from you at thecreativityinus@gmail.com. It has been a joy and pleasure to serve you through this book! I am grateful for your time!

Parting Prayer

LORD, bless the person experiencing this book. I pray You will open doors and provide insights where needed and convictions they heed to experience Your work in unleashing the creative power You have already deposited in them. May all be used for Your glory! In JESUS' name. Amen!

CPSIA information can be obtained
at www.ICGtesting.com
Printed in the USA
LVHW072223300123
738240LV00020B/653